Music, Style, and Aging

Music, Style, and Aging

GROWING OLD DISGRACEFULLY?

Andy Bennett

Temple University Press
Philadelphia

TEMPLE UNIVERSITY PRESS
Philadelphia, Pennsylvania 19122
www.temple.edu/tempress

Copyright © 2013 by Temple University
All rights reserved
Published 2013

Library of Congress Cataloging-in-Publication Data
Bennett, Andy, 1963–
 Music, style, and aging : growing old disgracefully? / Andy Bennett.
  p. cm.
 Includes bibliographical references and index.
 ISBN 978-1-4399-0807-5 (cloth : alk. paper) — ISBN 978-1-4399-0808-2
(pbk. : alk. paper) — ISBN 978-1-4399-0809-9 (e-book) 1. Popular
music—Social aspects. 2. Rock music—Social aspects. 3. Aging—Social
aspects. I. Title.
 ML3918.P67B44 2013
 781.64084'6—dc23

                                                    2012025884

♾ The paper used in this publication meets the requirements of the
American National Standard for Information Sciences—Permanence of
Paper for Printed Library Materials, ANSI Z39.48-1992

Printed in the United States of America

2 4 6 8 9 7 5 3 1

*For my father, George Herbert Bennett,
and to the memory of my mother,
Anne Shirley Bennett (1937–2008)*

Contents

Acknowledgments

This book has been some ten years in the making. During that time I have become a parent, lived and worked on three different continents, met many new and inspiring people, and grieved the passing of several people who were very dear to me. In today's academic world, ten years is undoubtedly a long period of time for the production of a monograph. All I can say in response to that is that this book is very much a product of particular circumstances; it has taken as long as it has taken to write, and in the ten years I have been working, the ideas informing the book have certainly moved around and changed (a bit like its author).

The idea for this book was hatched one night in September 2002 at a small music venue in East Kent where I had been invited to watch a local ska punk band. During the course of the evening, I happened to meet and have a drink with three aging punks. I no longer remember their names, but I will remain forever grateful to them for the delightful conversation we had and the formative ideas it generated for this book. I've met a great number of aging music fans since then and learned a lot about the ways in which music taste and age become tantalizingly intertwined. My thanks to all of those people in the United Kingdom, France, and Australia who agreed to be interviewed for this book—from Canterbury, to Lille, to Adelaide (and other places besides), the research for this project has been a real journey of discovery.

I would also like to acknowledge the support of my academic colleagues at the University of Surrey, Brock University, and Griffith University, the three institutions I have worked at while writing this book. I am indebted to a number of people in this respect but would like to say an especially big thank you to Paul Hodkinson, Geoff Cooper, Nicola Green, Sherill Dodds, Scott Henderson, Hans and Kathy Skott-Myhre, Ian Woodward, Margaret Gibson, Sarah Baker, and Christine Feldman. In addition to being fantastic people to work with, you have all shown a great deal of warmth and generosity of spirit.

Over the past ten years I have also had the privilege of working with some extremely gifted postdoctoral and postgraduate colleagues—Norman Urquia, Pete Webb, Mary Fogarty, Jodie Taylor, Alison Huber, Ian Rogers, Brady Robards, Raphael Nowak, Gavin Carfoot, Chris Driver, Lauren Istvandity, Eurico Viana Netto, William Lesitaokana, and Silvia Tarassi. Several of these people are now beginning to forge highly promising academic careers in their own right. Thanks to all of you for your support and for the invaluable insights you have given me into areas of contemporary cultural life that I previously had little familiarity with. A number of ideas resulting from our conversations over the years have found their way into this book.

While writing the book I have benefited from wonderful opportunities to travel and collect data interstate and overseas through generous visiting fellowships offered by the University of South Australia, the University of Lille, Curtin University, the University of Salford, and the University of Tallinn. Gerry Bloustien, Hervé Glevarec, Jon Stratton, George McKay, and Airi Alina Allaste have all been wonderfully supportive colleagues and great hosts during these visits. Several of these people have also taken time out of their busy careers to visit and contribute to the academic life of the Griffith Centre for Cultural Research. Additional visitors to the Centre who have also helped me forge ideas for this book include Les Back, Helen Thomas, Francois Matarasso, and Motti Regev. Thanks to all of you.

A very big note of thanks is reserved for my friend, colleague, and mentor Richard "Pete" Peterson, who, sadly, passed away in February

2010. As I have written elsewhere, Pete possessed a very special combination of qualities—gentle wit, warmth, and generosity, together with a high level of professionalism and academic rigor. All of this was topped with an intellectual curiosity and boundless energy for new ideas. I will never forget Pete's galvanizing call to action as we pulled together plans for our co-authored book *Music Scenes: Local, Translocal, and Virtual* (2004) back in July 2001 in my garden in Canterbury. Likewise, our afternoon whale-watching tour on Moreton Bay in September 2007 is a treasured memory. I miss you, Pete.

This book carries a dedication to my mother, Anne Shirley Bennett, who passed away in June 2008. Much of what I have achieved in my life and academic career could not have happened without her love and support. From the time I can remember listening to and enjoying music, Mum was someone whose interest in and enthusiasm for music was very inspirational. From her explanation of lyrics to songs such as "The Boxer" and "In the Ghetto" to helping me choose my first electric guitar and driving me to band practice when I was too young to drive myself, Mum was a big presence in my life. She had a keen interest in the subject matter of this book. I am sad that she didn't get to read it, but I am happy to have spent time talking to her about my ideas for the book.

Finally, big, big, big thanks to my wife, Monika, and my son, Daniel. Our life together is very special, and the magic you both bring to each and every day is so very much appreciated. We have shared so many adventures across the world and found a wonderful home together in southeast Queensland.

Music, Style, and Aging

Introduction

A Life-Changing Thing

I would hark back to, y'know, the birth of rock 'n' roll . . . and
Elvis Presley, an' you get something that hasn't happened before,
happening. Or perhaps, you get something happening which is,
ehm, a generational thing. I think in terms of music there are
pivotal times . . . the birth of rock 'n' roll, punk, hip-hop, rave,
for example . . . that so inspire a generation [such] that people are
fundamentally changed by this happening . . . but [among] certain
people who are susceptible to looking out for, y'know, something
new, eh, the actual change in their lives is phenomenal. It dictates
in a sense the rest of your life, because . . . the phenomen[on],
whatever happens, has such a fundamental effect on you that it
actually changes the course of your life. So, whereas it could be if
punk never happened or if, y'know, I was ten years older, I would
have perhaps missed out, or would have been led down different
avenues. But 'cause, y'know, it did feel like, yeah, [punk] was a life-
changing thing . . . an' I feel very privileged, as I think a lot of my
contemporaries were, to [have] be[en] around at the time, when
this was happening. (English male punk, aged forty-four)

The beginning of the twenty-first century marks an interesting
and highly significant period in contemporary popular music
history. Almost every living generation in the Westernized
world has grown up in an age during which popular music has been a
pivotal element of the global media and cultural industries, be it the
advent of rock 'n' roll during the mid-1950s, the psychedelic and politicized rock of the late 1960s, the punk backlash of the mid-1970s, or
the dance music explosion of the late 1980s. The sounds, styles, and
cultural impact of each of these popular music eras have been vividly documented in books, magazine articles, motion pictures, and

television series. Indeed, such accounts of popular music's impact on youth and the wider society now form part of our general understanding of the cultural changes that swept through Western nations after 1950.

Far less well documented, however, are the more long-term effects on those individuals who passed through this "youthquake" (Leech 1973) on their way to adulthood. In 1983, Simon Frith suggested that "the sociology of rock is inseparable from the sociology of youth" (1983: 9). This statement may have been an astute observation at the time but today it appears more problematic. What is missing from Frith's observation—and something that has come to register ever more critically in the thirty years since it was made—is a sense of what happens to popular music audiences beyond the time of their youth—and whether musical tastes acquired as teenagers actively influence or shape subsequent biographical trajectories. Frith, of course, is not alone in this respect. In most academic and popular accounts of music and youth, the liminality of youth as a life stage and what subsequently becomes of those involved in music-driven youth cultures have never really been primary points for consideration.

This book constitutes an attempt to deal precisely with the question of how people move on from youth and effectively grow older with popular music. The book's starting point examines the notion that the cultural significance of popular music is no longer tied exclusively to youth and, for many people, the music that "mattered" to them in their youth continues to play an important role in their adult lives. Such importance, it is argued, goes well beyond the often cited "nostalgia value" of popular music. Rather than portraying a group of individuals yearning for a return to the days of their youth, I illustrate that aging audiences for popular music often exhibit a dynamic, shifting, and developing quality in their appreciation of music, its relevance to their everyday lives, and its broader sociocultural significance. It is further explained how, for many aging followers of rock, punk, dance, and other contemporary popular music genres, the cultural sensibilities they acquired as members of music-driven youth cultures have remained with them, shaping their life courses and becoming ingrained in their biographical trajectories and associated lifestyle sensibilities.

The book does not claim that a particular style of music will have the "same" effect on everyone, nor does it maintain that music continues to matter in the same way, or to the same degree, in each individual case. In conducting the research for this study, I encountered numerous people who described themselves as "ex" rockers, hippies, punks, and so on, the "ex" clearly demarcating this stage of their lives as something they felt they had left behind, something they regarded as an aspect of their "youth," with no obvious ongoing significance to their post-youth lives. In one extreme example, a former punk, now in her mid-forties and living in northern France, claimed that trying to maintain an interest in punk beyond her teens would have been incompatible with the punk ethos, the latter connoting an "instant music and philosophy."[1] At the same time, however, I also encountered a significant number of middle-aged popular music fans who did continue to identify themselves as hippies, punks, and so on. For these people, music and the associated lifestyle traits and/or ideologies that go with it have continued to matter in their lives in substantial ways and, in a number of cases, had a considerable impact on the direction of their lives in the intervening years since their youth.

I do not wish to suggest either that the topic of individuals aging with music is in any way exclusively associated with the musical and cultural genres examined in this book. The legions of aging jazz and swing fans are testimony to the established importance of music in people's lives across generations and genres. Similarly, in their work on social dance in the third age, Cooper and Thomas argue that "social dance for older people, as for the young, produces and preserves a superior, symbolic generational identity" (2002: 703). I do, however, want to argue that the musical and associated cultural and stylistic examples chosen for study in this book mark a significant turning point in the history of Western popular music. I say this because these examples are all rooted in an era of burgeoning consumerism and mediatization in which connections between music and identity found a new level of immediacy. At the same time, the ways in which popular music were consumed and experienced from the early 1950s onward

---

1. Interview originally conducted in French with assistance from Hervé Glevarec. English translation provided by Hervé Glevarec.

opened up an ever-increasing universe of possibilities for the reflexive understanding and use of popular music as a cultural resource in everyday life.

The book's exploration of aging popular music audiences is presented in six chapters and divided into two main parts. Part I, comprising Chapters 1 and 2, seeks to contextualize the aging popular music audience both empirically and theoretically.

Chapter 1 begins by considering existing representations of aging popular music fans as they figure in journalistic and, to some extent, academic accounts. It is observed how such representations often rely on crudely devised labels, such as "old hippie" and, more recently, the "fifty quid man," to describe aging music fans and their cultural practices as essentially deviant. Such labels, it is argued, rely on an ageist discourse that paints a highly stereotypical and one-sided picture of the meaning of popular music in aging fans' lives.

The chapter then begins the task of remapping the sociocultural context of the aging popular music audience. In doing so, the chapter draws on the cultural sociological perspectives offered by Chaney (1996, 2002) and Giddens (1991) relating to reflexivity and identity in late modernity and applies these to the small extant literature on aging, consumerism, and popular culture. It is argued that, as with earlier stages in the life course, aging identities are now increasingly derived through texts, images, and other mediated leisure forms. Moving then to a discussion of how the music industry, together with other associated cultural industries, has responded to an aging consumer base, it is suggested that the objects, images, and texts produced with aging consumers in mind have a significance that goes well beyond their "nostalgia value." Thus, it is contested, for individuals who came of age in the burgeoning consumer society of the 1950s and 1960s and who thus take consumer lifestyles for granted as a part of their everyday cultural milieu, consumption of products such as CD reissues of classic albums, DVD versions of classic rock performances, and attendance at tribute band concerts need not merely constitute, as is often suggested, a nostalgic "harking back" to the time of one's youth. Rather, it is argued, such investment illustrates the way in which music has become an integral part of individual identity; music serves as a cultural backdrop for aging fans' lives in many ways, informing a variety of social sensibilities that include, for example, the visual representation of the aging identity, choice of career path, relationships with family and peers, and political outlook. The prevalence of music in such contexts, it is suggested, relates in part to the loosening hold of traditional structural factors on individuals and the increasing importance of popular cultural resources as a means of forging and articulating social identities. Also significant, however, is the aging process itself. As music fans age, it is suggested, the meaning and significance of music become more steadily and subtly ingrained in their identities, to the extent that the "spectacular" forms of collective allegiance to musical styles often exhibited by younger fans become much less important than the personal connection one feels to music as an inspirational resource. For many aging fans, the experience of music becomes highly personal, its meaning interwoven with the biographical development of the individual. The final section of Chapter 1 extends this argument through an examination of the relationship between popular music, aging, and gender.

Chapter 2 provides theoretical models through which to investigate and interpret the relationship between popular music, aging, and identity. The chapter explores the work of Frith (1987) and DeNora (2000), which addresses the importance of music for individuals in mundane, everyday contexts. Such work, addressing as it does issues of biography, memory, and aesthetics, offers a particularly fertile starting point for an investigation of the highly personal, often complex introspective accounts of music meaning offered by individual aging music fans and the ways in such accounts map onto and are articulated by the aging process itself.

Later in the chapter, these ideas are linked with the concept of lifestyle as a means of illustrating how such individualized responses to music and its cultural resonances nonetheless cohere into collective forms of cultural practice. Using Chaney's (1996) concept of lifestyle sites and strategies, I argue that aging music audiences produce, manage, and articulate identities through the appropriation, inscription, and representation of musical texts and associated resources into lifestyle projects that bond and cohere into collective forms of cultural practice. The resultant clusters of collective cultural practice, it is subsequently argued, can be most effectively theorized by drawing on Peterson and Bennett's (2004) three-tier model of music scenes—"local," "translocal," and "virtual." In addition to allowing for the possibility of clusters of aging music fans who continue to use local networks of venues, bars, and record shops as gathering spaces, Peterson and Bennett's emphasis on the transnational and virtual elements of scene also allows for more temporal and individualized forms of fan practice that, as this book demonstrates, are often evident among older popular music fans. Finally, a new category, "affective scene," is introduced as a means of further finessing Peterson and Bennett's model and its applicability to the sociocultural context of the aging music audience.

Part II comprises four ethnographic case-study chapters focusing on specific aspects of the relationship between popular music, aging, and lifestyle.

Chapter 3 examines issues of visual appearance and body image among aging music audiences, looking specifically at the way fashion, hairstyle, and forms of body modification associated with particular genres of music are either managed or modified when music fans reach middle age and begin to contemplate later life. The chapter illustrates how, in keeping with other aspects of individual identity in late modernity, the aging body has become a reflexively articulated and individually constructed project. As illustrated, for many aging popular music fans, the process of aging has brought with it a new attitude toward visual image, one that downplays the visual with a new emphasis on the importance of more introspective, aesthetically situated sensibilities in relation to music and its impact on the life course. Thus, in the case of aging punks, who form a large part of the empirical case-study material presented in Chapter 3, if visual image was once a highly important aspect of their punk credentials, for many the need to "dress" punk has been replaced by a more introspective subscription to the punk ethos. The punk ethos allows for a more dressed down and, in some cases, barely discernible visual punk image. In justifying this modification of their visual image, older punks argue that their internalization of the punk message and worldview over the years has rendered the need for a visually obvious persona.

Chapter 4 considers the relationship between musical taste and choice of career path. Thus far, there has been little acknowledgment in the academic literature of this relationship, the exception being studies of local music scenes that have focused on music-making itself and/or related activities as a form of work and possible route into the world of professional music-making. As Chapter 4 illustrates, however, music has had more far-reaching effects on the ways in which some aging fans have chosen careers and/or structured their working lives. Thus, for some older music fans, a long-term interest in music has led them to pursue what could broadly be referred to as "alternative" careers. For example, a number of aging punks embrace a strong DIY (do-it-yourself) aesthetic, eschewing "nine-to-five" jobs and opting instead for self-made career paths that incorporate personal interests and lifestyle-related work projects. In other cases, a long-term interest in music has motivated some aging fans to become proactive in the preservation of particular music genres or in the dissemination of musical skills—for example, through launching independent record labels or working for local community projects aimed at providing music-making facilities and training for socioeconomically disadvantaged youth. At other times, aging music fans working in more mainstream occupations have purposely chosen career paths that allow space and flexibility for continuing engagement with and participation in music-related practices that can be fitted in around a work schedule.

Chapter 5 focuses on issues of continuity and conflict among different generations of music fans. Although the primary purpose of this book is to examine the lifestyles and identities of aging music fans, as the ethnographic research conducted for the book illustrated to me, a number of aging fans continue to associate with music scenes that also attract younger people. It was also clear from the research that the nature of the relationship between aging music fans and their younger peers varies a great deal. Thus, some aging fans regard themselves as forefathers or mentors whose task is to oversee the development of newer, younger members of those music scenes in which they participate. This role may take a variety of forms, from imparting the "correct" cultural sensibilities to providing hands-on knowledge and know-how—as, for example, with aging members of a dance music collective who offer young dance music fans the opportunity to learn about the practicalities of staging dance parties. Family life and responsibility for children have also acted as a driver for some aging fans to rethink and, in some cases, create new spaces for engagement with the dance party scene. The increasingly multigenerational nature of the mainstream music industry is also creating new sensibilities of age—and age acceptance—within local music-making scenes, as evidenced by the account of several interviewees regarding their involvement in multigenerational rock and pop bands. Finally, the chapter considers how parents and children often communicate via the medium of music—sharing ideas about music and trading musical tastes with each other. As is illustrated, such musicalized dialogues can often be an important source of bonding between parents and children.

Chapter 6 addresses the long-term influence of popular music on the political orientation and worldview of aging music fans, assessing the extent to which the ideologies of power, resistance, and defiance, as generated through particular musics, remain with and are adapted by fans as they grow older. The chapter first examines the long-term impact of politicized rock and its associated countercultural ideology among members of the baby-boomer generation, many of whom still continue to self-identify as hippies. Issues explored include how the political messages of rock, often cited as of key significance to hippie audiences in the 1960s, are perceived by some of those same "aging" hippies today. Also reviewed are the more long-term spiritual impacts of music from the countercultural era on aging baby-boomer listeners. I then discuss the legacy of punk ideology, as communicated through the music, for those who embraced it as teenagers and early twentysomethings. I show that punk politics continue to play an important role in the lives of many aging punks. Within this discussion, it is also considered how the concept of anarchy, once a prominent byword for punk's alternative political aspirations, has been reassessed by many older punks, who now view it as an overly negative and, in many ways, naive statement. Many older punks thus convey how the subversiveness of their punk youth has matured over the years into a more tolerant and worldly outlook, something that they feel sits well with an aging punk persona.

The conclusion of the book offers a series of speculative observations on how the aging baby-boomer and post-boomer generations' transition from middle age to later life will bring with it new perceptions of eldership. Drawing on a collection of observations offered by aging music fans interviewed for this book, I show how, through their collective perceptions of what it means to grow old, baby-boomer and post-boomer generations bring with them new sets of demands and expectations regarding the quality of life in the third age. These expectations are assessed not merely in terms of access to basic facilities—food, clothing, shelter, hygiene, and so on—but also with reference to the preservation of those leisure and lifestyle resources that form the foundations upon which late modern identity and everyday culture are established.

I / Contextualizing Popular Music and Aging

1 / Popular Music and the Aging Audience

In June 1996, when veteran U.K. punk rockers the Sex Pistols performed their twentieth-anniversary reunion concert at London's Finsbury Park, early into the band's set lead singer John Lydon (alias Johnny Rotten) is reputed to have said to the audience, "Forty, fat, and back!"[1] Offered as a self-mocking remark by Lydon on the aging profile of the Sex Pistols, this comment was also a timely reflection on the longevity of punk and its aging fan base. Along with the younger fans who were there to see a punk legend for the first—and possibly last—time, there were also many "older" punks, people in their forties and fifties who were first drawn to punk during their late teens or early twenties and have remained followers of the music ever since. Lydon is not alone in drawing attention to the aging demographic of rock performers and their audiences in this way. During a February 2005 concert at the Thebarton Theatre in Adelaide, South Australia, stalwart female rocker Suzi Quatro, now in her mid-fifties, remarked that it was her twenty-first Australian tour and, following expressions of surprise and adulation from the audience, exclaimed,

---

1. As reported to me by a Sex Pistols fan who was present at the event.

"Yeah, we grew up together, right?"[2] Again, Quatro's comments are significant in that they acknowledge the continuing importance of popular music for people well into middle age and beyond. And yet, for all the anecdotal evidence that aging popular music fans continue to take their music, and themselves, very seriously, little attempt has been made, in academic writing or elsewhere, to engage with the phenomenon of the aging popular music audience. When aging music fans are written about, more often than not it is in a negative or tongue-in-cheek way, in which they are referred to as has-beens, overgrown teenagers, and the like. As this chapter illustrates, however, such accounts are increasingly out of step with a world in which definitions of aging and generational boundaries are radically shifting. Where once rigid social divisions were drawn between adolescence, early adulthood, middle age, and later life, in late modernity such divisions are much less evident as the lifestyles of people at each of these stages of life become more similar.

A further problem with popular representations of aging music audiences is the tendency to equate middle-aged music fandom with a nostalgic harking back to the time of one's youth. Again, however, it could be argued that such representations are both essentialist and overly simplistic. Although nostalgia may be one contributing factor to a continuing personal investment in popular music in middle age and beyond, arguably it is by no means the only factor. Indeed, as this book endeavors to illustrate, many aging popular music fans live very much in the present, music having informed their biographies in ways that significantly shape current and ongoing aspects of their everyday lives.

The key purpose of this chapter, then, is to contextualize the aging popular music audience in late modernity and to begin sketching out the ways in which popular music informs issues of aging lifestyle, and biography in a late modern context. In the first instance, however, it is useful to consider, and to begin deconstructing, some of the dominant representations of aging music fans that abound in the popular media and are occasionally found in academically informed writing.

---

2. Drawn from my own field notes made while attending this concert.

Aging Rockers! Popular Stereotypes of Aging Music Audiences

There are numerous stereotypes describing popular music fans in middle age and beyond, "old hippie" and "aging rocker" being two of the most widely used.

The media in particular appear to revel in the use of such stereotypes. Represented as typically male and hopelessly immature, the aging music fan is often portrayed by the media as a cultural misfit—a dysfunctional, middle-aged individual longing for a return to the days of his youth. Such a sentiment is clear in the following review of a concert performed by enduring hard rock band AC/DC at London's Hammersmith Apollo:

> When the house lights finally dimmed the cheers almost gave the venue an unwanted extension as grown men transformed into the teenagers they were when they first memorised every lyric and riff were blasted by the unmistakable sound of AC/DC powering through "Hell Ain't A Bad Place To Be", imaginary full heads of hair were banged and air guitars were played everywhere.[3]

At one level, such depictions of aging music fans can be read in a quasi-functionalist way as an attempt on the part of the media to address the issue of "correct" and "incorrect" roles in society. Thus, aging music fans are effectively being labeled or "stereotyped" as "too old" to legitimately engage in such forms of fan behavior. Pickering suggests that the act of stereotyping functions to "reduce specific groups and categories to a limited set of conceptions" (2001: 10). The application of stereotypes is thus instrumental in ascribing particular sets of characteristics and mannerisms to certain groups and individuals and may also result in their stigmatization by the wider society. This is a particularly accurate description of the way in which aging music audiences are portrayed by the media. Not quite "folk devils"

---

3. *Tiscali Reviews*, www.tiscali.co.uk/music/reviews/031023_ac_dc.html (accessed May 10, 2004).

(Cohen 1987) of the late modern era, "aging rockers" are neverthe-less portrayed in the media as essentially deviant and thus socially unacceptable.

Moreover, it is not only aging music audiences who are repre-sented in this way; the artists admired by such audiences often find themselves the subjects of such media stigmatization as well. For ex-ample, in a *Sunday Times* article entitled "Livin' Dull," journalist Jer-emy Langmead observes:

> In the old days, rock stars used to become immortal, and then choke on their own vomit and expire, and it was neat, ironic and pleasing. Not any more. Today they refuse to retire. They do not even have the manners to just GO AWAY. Here they are on *Top Of The Pops*, lumbering about with their bovine songs, imbecile lyrics and hairdon'ts from hell. . . . What is going on? Hasn't Rod Stewart heard of Jimi Hendrix? Didn't Roger "Hope I Die Before I Get Old" Daltry pay any attention to his own lyrics? Can't Eric Clapton remember Jim Morri-son? (1994: 18)

In more recent times, such representations of the "aging rocker" have taken a new twist in the form of MTV's reality sitcom *The Os-bournes*, which focuses on the day-to-day domestic life of veteran heavy metal singer Ozzy Osbourne, his manager-wife Sharon, and their two teenage children, Jack and Kelly (see Kompare 2004). Al-though the show focuses evenly on all four members of the Osbourne family, the portrayal of Ozzy Osbourne's "aging rocker" profile and struggle to balance domesticity with his rock 'n' roll lifestyle is clearly intended as a key aspect of the show's entertainment value. The spec-tacle of Osbourne as a middle-aged husband and father trying to come to terms with his wife's obsession with her numerous pet dogs and his children's temper tantrums is portrayed as being comically out of step with the notoriety of his black magic–inspired song lyrics, legendary on-stage antics, and reputation as the "Prince of Darkness." In this respect, Osbourne's willingness to parody himself is a crucial ingredient in the success of *The Osbournes* concept. Equally impor-tant, however, are the stock representations of the family structure—

and the roles of individual family members within this—on which *The Osbournes* trades. The representations of family life in *The Osbournes*, despite the obvious eccentricities of the four characters involved, are grounded in an essentially "traditional" understanding of the nuclear family as a social institution.

During the past few years, a new stereotype of the aging music fan—the "fifty quid man"—has entered the vocabulary of the media journalist. The "fifty quid man" describes an apparently growing trait among middle-aged, professional men of spending large amounts of their disposable income on music products. According to recent media reports, the fifty quid man, so named because of his average weekly spending in the record shop, has significantly boosted the revenue of the music industry. In March 2004, the British newspaper the *Guardian* ran a feature on the phenomenon of the fifty quid man, citing British entertainment industry figure David Hepworth, who first defined the term:

> On a hot day at County Hall in London, Hepworth stood up and gave Britain's record-company bosses a lecture about their own customers, concentrating on "the 50-quid guy,"[4] a term he had picked up from friends in retail. "This is the guy we've all seen in Borders or HMV on a Friday afternoon, possibly after a drink or two, tie slightly undone, buying two CDs, a DVD and maybe a book—fifty quid's worth—and frantically computing how he's going to convince his partner that this is a really, really worthwhile investment."[5]

The fifty quid man fits well with the media's gallery of stereotypes to describe aging music fans. His lifestyle—upwardly mobile, affluent, and middle-aged—is comically contrasted with his ongoing, youth-like "obsession" with music. Indeed, affluence and domesticity

---

4. Although Hepworth refers here to the "50-quid guy," the more commonly used expression is "fifty quid man," hence the use of the latter term in this chapter.

5. De Lisle, T. (2004). Melody maker, *The Guardian*, March 1. Available at http://www.guardian.co.uk/arts/features/story/0,11710,1159112,00.html (accessed April 21, 2005).

are frequently highlighted in media accounts of aging music fans, the implied irony here being that rock music, once the signature tune of disenfranchised, disempowered, angry youth, is now the bedfellow of the socially and economically empowered middle-aged professional. Such individuals, it is argued, have sensationally lost the "rock" plot, to the extent that they literally treat rock concert outings as a family picnic. Thus, as *Mojo* journalist Mark Ellen observed in relation to the audience for the 1996 Hyde Park concert in London, whose head-lining acts included Eric Clapton and Bob Dylan, "for every guitar-toting hippy [*sic*] in an ethnic weave there's a hamper-laden family of four savouring a fresh baguette and a ripe French cheese" (1996: 110). From the point of view of such reports, becoming middle-aged, professional, and family-centered is incompatible with an apprecia-tion of rock music's alleged deeper social resonance. The older fan is thus reduced to the status of "music tourist." Stripped of the presumed angst and desperation that drove them to listen to particular artists and musics during their youth, fifty-something "aging rockers" are deemed to consume music in much the same way as they consume any other "product"—no musical outing being complete without the lavish home comforts to which they have become accustomed. This sentiment is clearly captured in the following extract from an article in the British newspaper the *Times* regarding the recently revived Isle of Wight Festival:[6] "Within days of David Bowie and the Who being confirmed as top billers, the best hotels on the island were besieged by ageing rockers with money."[7] The irony present in this comment again underscores a broader, and essentially ageist, assumption that rock festivals are no place for well-heeled, middle-aged professionals afraid of roughing it for a weekend in the "true" festival spirit.

It is not only in the media, however, that such disparaging ac-counts of aging popular music fans are to be found. In the academic literature too, occasional references to aging audiences for various

---

6. The first Isle of Wight Festival was held in 1968 and was followed by two more festivals in 1969 and 1970 (see Hinton 1995).

7. *Times Online.* Available at www.timesonline.co.uk/article/0,4161-1026062,00. html (accessed May 10, 2004).

post-1950s popular music genres often contain observations that are essentially negative in tone. For example, in her otherwise highly compelling study of heavy metal, Deena Weinstein notes:

> Adults who continue to appreciate metal rarely use the metal media, except for playing their old albums. They do not attend many, if any concerts; do not buy new metal releases or metal magazines; and do not call in requests on the radio. Many do not even play their albums all that much, but they have not thrown them out either. Once part of the metal subculture, they are now like wistful emigrants, living a continent away in another world than their own. (2000: 111)

Weinstein's notion that aging heavy metal fans occupy a cultural limbo land, unable to connect in any palpable sense with the contemporary metal scene and yet simultaneously out of touch with the reality of their adult lives, is reinforced by Andrew Ross's similarly pathological representation of the aging baby-boomer generation in his introduction to mid-1990s youth and music anthology *Microphone Fiends*. Thus, observes Ross: "It is not just Mick Jagger and Tina Turner who imagine themselves to be eighteen years old and steppin' out; a significant mass of baby boomers partially act out this belief in their daily lives" (1994: 8).

Taken together, journalistic and academic accounts such as these assume an unproblematic equation between "legitimate" popular music fandom and age, popular music fandom being cast as the cultural practice of sixteen- to twenty-five-year-olds. Or, perhaps more accurately, such accounts imply a "natural" generational divide between the pleasures of popular music fandom and the responsibilities of adult life. With age, it is assumed, individuals grow out of their rock, punk, and other "alternative" identities and assume identities and attendant musical tastes more attuned to their status as mature, responsible "adults." Thus, according to *Sunday Times* journalist Jeremy Langmead: "The point is that both rock 'n' roll and its little cousin, pop, were made for the young. Old people have opera, [Andrew] Lloyd Webber and theme tunes" (1994: 18). Such assumptions, however, seem odd ones to make given that popular music—

in the contemporary sense of the term—now has a history spanning over fifty years. Indeed, it is not merely the music but also the way it has been mediated and consumed from 1955 onward that is significant in this respect. Thus, as Savage (1990) notes, every generation in the Westernized world born during or after the 1940s has been effectively trained in the age of consumerism, their lifestyles and identities based on a series of consumption practices, in which popular music has played a key role. One might reasonably expect then that where investment in a musical style has been particularly intensive during one's teenage to twenty-something years such investment may well continue well into middle age and beyond. The fact that an individual becomes a follower of a style of music as a "young" person may matter far less than what that music continues to mean to them as they grow older.

The preservation of taste in music and other popular cultural forms among aging music fans in this way can be linked to the broader changes in attitude toward aging and the life course in late modernity and the influence of the media and cultural industries upon these changes. The increasing role of the media and cultural industries in the representation of the aging body and the concomitant articulation of an aging identity have led to significant shifts in the way people think about and conceptualize the aging process. A major consequence of this is that once clearly defined divisions between generations in terms of leisure patterns and lifestyle preferences are becoming increasingly blurred.

As Old as You Feel: Aging and Late Modernity

As recent work on aging and the life course illustrates, despite being universally accepted as a biological inevitability, aging is very much a socially and historically constructed concept. Thus, as Featherstone and Hepworth observe:

> Whilst the biological processes of aging, old age and death cannot in the last resort be avoided, the meanings which we give to these processes and the evaluations we make of people

as they grow physically older are social constructions which reflect the beliefs and values found in a specific culture at a particular period in history. (1995: 30–31)

Similarly, Blaikie asserts that "ageing is made to appear self-evident, an inevitable aspect of the human condition, when, in fact, it is also a profoundly sociological and historical construct" (1999: 5). Looking at aging in the context of Western industrial societies, Featherstone and Hepworth note how the weight of social conventions and expectations attached to aging was such that individuals were effectively forced to "become" old. As a consequence, claim Featherstone and Hepworth, dominant traditional images of aging were less a representation of the individual's perceived self than "a mask which conceal[ed] the essential identity of the person beneath" (1991: 379).

With the onset of late modernity in contemporary society, such conventions of aging and the expectations that these place on the individual have been increasingly thrown into question. Previously dominant discourses on aging have been challenged by alternative representations of aging generated by the media, cultural industries, and other dominant social institutions. Giddens (1991) and Chaney (1996, 2002) have argued that a key effect of the inroads made by the media and cultural industries into the fabric of everyday life has been the fostering of a reflexivity on the part of individuals who now effectively "choose" their identities rather than these being imposed through the structured experience of class, gender, and ethnicity. Indeed, Chaney has gone so far as to suggest that the media and popular culture industries have become primary referents for individuals in this respect, replacing structural influences as forms of cultural authority through which individuals construct and articulate their social identities. Thus, observes Chaney:

If we have been forced into more personal choices about what to believe, there is likely to be a greater demand for new sorts of expertise and guidance. And thus a paradoxical intensification of the social process of reflexivity is a proliferation of expertise and authority in fragmented culture. The reason why a more intense reflexivity is associated with greater uniformity becomes clearer if it is appreciated that the processes of heightened reflexive consciousness are articulated through textually mediated discourses more generally.[8] (2002: 24)

It follows that if such "textually mediated discourses" are becoming increasingly central to the ways in which individuals frame their identity, then this factor will be evident throughout the life course to the extent that even the concept of "aging" may be understood in a plurality of ways rather than the singular and essentialist meaning of "becoming old." Indeed, as Featherstone and Hepworth observe, the fact that the aging process itself is now a textually mediated discourse is demonstrated quite palpably by "the near impossibility of avoiding images of aging and old age in the cinema, television, radio, novels, magazines and newspapers" (1995: 29).

One notable effect of this mediatization process is that the negativity that was once associated with aging has gradually been replaced by more "positive" images of aging and the life course (Featherstone and Hepworth 1995). In the context of late modernity, aging is no longer regarded simply as a slow and inevitable process of bodily decay and deterioration. On the contrary, it is often regarded as a time of personal growth and even rejuvenation. Thus, as Hunt observes in relation to those currently in middle age and contemplating later life: "These are people who know that they have another 30–40 years of life expectancy ahead of them. They may see a practically endless future rather than the beginning of the end" (2005: 183). Certainly, as people age, the likelihood of poor health, infirmity, and other factors that may prevent them from pursuing a desired lifestyle increases. At the same time, however, improving standards of health and the availability of treatments to enable those with long-term illnesses and age-related disabilities to lead relatively normal lives have given individuals higher levels of expectation that they will be able to have

---

8. The impact of media and consumerism on biographical trajectory and generational change has a longer history, as illustrated, for example, by Riesman's ([1950] 2001) *The Lonely Crowd*. In the mid-twentieth century, however, such traits were considered evidence of societal anomie rather than a positive facilitator of individual reflexivity and biographical development.

the sort of life they choose in middle age and later life (Cunningham-Burley and Backett-Milburn 1998). This is supported by Timmer, Bode, and Dittman-Kohl's study of expected gains by individuals during the second half of life. Many of those involved in the research anticipated and, in many cases, actively worked toward capitalizing on their personal interests and leisure preferences, spending time with their loved ones, and generally improving their quality of life. As Timmer, Bode, and Dittman-Kohl observe: "The majority of gain anticipations refer[red] to making day-to-day life more enjoyable; to planning new projects such as travelling; to intensifying social relationships; and to self-development" (2003: 16).

Consuming Aging Identities

In recent years, a sizable cultural industry has grown up around the promotion and consumption of more positive images of aging and associated lifestyles. Thus, for example, a growing number of books and magazines are dedicated to discussing lifestyle options—dress, food, holiday destinations, sporting activities, and so on—for an aging readership (see Featherstone and Hepworth 1995; McHugh 2003). Likewise, the opportunity to take early retirement has spurred an increase in travel and migration among those in middle age and later life. As McHugh notes, so many retired people now seek to relocate, either within their own country or overseas, that the trend has sparked a highly lucrative retirement industry supported by a dedicated media: "*Where to Retire?*—a popular magazine title—is not an idle question. It encapsulates the lifeblood of the burgeoning retirement industry and the secret to longevity for retirees who seek the fountain of agelessness" (2003: 166). McHugh goes on to note the growing number of local organizations and business ventures now geared toward "selling" their particular region "to healthy and wealthy retirees and pre-retirees" (2003: 166).

Similarly, a proliferation of media personalities, television celebrities, and film stars who continue to be "youthful" and physically active despite their age serve as significant role models in an aging society. Blaikie notes how "films featuring older people in leading roles have been designed to attract older audiences, and some—*Driving*

Miss Daisy, Trip to Bountiful, On Golden Pond, Cocoon—have enjoyed commercial good fortune partly because of their upbeat messages of self-actualisation and rejuvenation" (1999: 95). In the world of fashion too, changing social perceptions of aging and lifestyle have had a marked effect on the industry's understanding of the relationship between clothing, image, identity, and age. Whereas traditionally individuals have been expected to comply with particular conventions of dress that confirmed their age and status (Lurie 1981), today there is a blurring of dress conventions that extends across the generations. As an example of this, Featherstone and Hepworth observe: "There is an increasing similarity in modes of presentation of self, gestures and postures, fashions and leisure time pursuits adopted by both parents and their children, and some movement can be seen towards a more informal uni-age style" (1991: 372).

Such blurring of generational boundaries in terms of fashion and style preferences has had a pronounced effect on the marketing strategies of the major clothing companies. As Blaikie observes, "Many advertisers and designers are already gearing up for major shifts in market orientation as inter-generational marketing appeal comes into its own" (1999: 103). As an indication of this trend, Blaikie cites the Levi's jeans company's use of older models—between the ages of sixty and eighty-six—in television commercials promoting its products.

The music industry has also become increasingly aware of the shifting demography of its market and has adapted accordingly. If the media and cultural industries have produced a series of iconic reference points for aging consumers, then veteran music artists such as Bob Dylan, Paul McCartney, and the Rolling Stones have played a key role in this respect. During the 1960s, the appeal of these artists centered on the sense of affinity that their then teen audience felt for them. As Plasketes and Plasketes observe: "There existed a strong bond between performer and audience, because there was the sense that the stars were not being imposed from above but had sprung up from similar ranks as the audience" (1987: 30). Today, Dylan, McCartney, and the Stones continue to command large numbers of loyal supporters, many of whom are long-term fans and have essentially aged along with these artists. Indeed, if Dylan, McCartney, and the Stones were trendsetters in the 1960s, then they can equally be regarded as trendsetters today, and for reasons not entirely different from those that first propelled them to stardom. These and other artists continue to act as spokespeople for the baby-boomer generation. In the 1960s, the baby-boomer generation was concerned with forging its own distinctive, collective identity through the attachment of a new series of meanings to youth (Chambers 1985). Today, that same generation is taking another step into the cultural unknown, as the first fully mediatized and consumer-centered generation to have reached middle age and now be contemplating the "third age." As members of this generation search for cultural resources and role models through which to construct and articulate their aging identities, Dylan, McCartney, and the Stones, together with a variety of other rock and pop icons now in their fifties and early sixties, continue to act as significant role models. Most importantly, such artists provide and promote a series of critical indicators and visual/aesthetic points of reference as to the construction and presentation of aging baby-boomer identities.

This ongoing connection between baby-boomer rock artists and their aging audience has been facilitated largely by a vociferous marketing strategy on the part of the music industry that targets the tastes of its aging baby-boomer consumer base. Since the mid-1990s, a large-scale retro market has blossomed. Compact discs (CDs), videos, and, more recently, digital video discs (DVDs) featuring previously unreleased studio and live material from a range of sixties and seventies rock artists, including Jimi Hendrix, the Doors, and Led Zeppelin, have been made commercially available for the first time. Similarly, the year 1995 saw the release of *The Beatles Anthology* television documentary series. In the six-part series, the then three surviving members of the Beatles, Paul McCartney, George Harrison, and Ringo Starr, were brought together for the first time in over twenty-five years to be interviewed, individually and together, about their experiences as the Beatles. Together with original Beatles producer George Martin, McCartney, Harrison, and Starr also collaborated in the studio, compiling studio outtakes of Beatles material for the six-CD *Beatles Anthology* collection and working on two new Beatles songs, "Free as a Bird" and "Real Love." For the new songs, they utilized "demo" recordings[9] made by fellow Beatle John Lennon before his murder in New York City in December 1980.[10] Both songs featured Lennon's original vocal tracks, which, with the use of new digital recording and editing techniques, were lifted directly from his homemade demo recordings and set to new arrangements. During the same period, full-length film versions of legendary late sixties and early seventies rock festivals such as Monterey[11] and Isle of Wight were released, and in 1994 *Woodstock: The Director's Cut* restored a number of performances, notably those by Canned Heat and the Jefferson Airplane, edited from the original version of the film released in 1970 (see Bennett 2004a).

The mid-1990s also saw the launch of retro-music magazines *Mojo* and *Classic Rock*, both of which routinely feature lengthy retrospective pieces on the most celebrated rock artists of the 1960s, 1970s, and, increasingly, the 1980s. Similarly, in 1993 Richard Branson's Virgin organization introduced its own radio station in the shape of Virgin 1215 (now Virgin FM). Promoted in the United Kingdon as an alternative to BBC Radio 1—which had recently restaffed with a younger generation of DJs and introduced playlists dominated by dance and rap music in order to preserve its image as a youth-music station—Virgin proclaimed itself a station dedicated to playing "classic tracks and the best new music" (new music in this case being new releases by established rock and pop artists or newer artists whose music was characterized by rock, blues, and soul influences). The tele-

---

9. The term "demo," shorthand for "demonstration tape," refers to a basic version of a newly composed song—typically consisting of vocal/guitar or piano/guitar—recorded by the composer as a means of conveying the essence of the song to fellow musicians.

10. Both "Free as a Bird" and "Real Love" were co-produced by the then three surviving Beatles and former Electric Light Orchestra front man Jeff Lynne. John Lennon is also given a production credit because of his initial composition of the songs and creation of the demos on which the finished songs are based.

11. In 2002, the 1968 film *Monterey Pop*, documenting the 1967 Monterey Pop Festival, was released as a box set that included two hours of extra performance footage and two additional short films, also by producer D. A. Pennebaker, *Jimi Plays Monterey* and *Shake! Otis at Monterey* (both of which had originally been released in 1986).

vision industry has also increasingly turned its eye on the aging baby-boomer audience as seen, for example, with the mid-1990s *Dancing in the Streets* (a ten-part documentary series focusing on the development of postwar popular music from the 1950s to the early 1990s) and, more recently, the *Classic Albums* series. Similarly, both radio and television regularly feature documentaries and one-off retrospectives focusing on particular popular music artists and/or genres from the 1950s onward.

The efforts of the music and entertainment industries in servicing the tastes of the aging baby-boomer and post-baby-boomer generations and accurately predicting the expansion of this market have borne fruit. As an article in the British newspaper the *Guardian* reported in 2005:

> According to recent figures from the British Phonographic Industry (BPI), the 12-to-19 age group accounted for 16.4% of album sales in 2002, a sharp fall on 2000 (22.1%), while 40- to 49-year-olds went the other way, rising from 16.5% to 19.1%. Buyers in their 50s (14.3%) are not far behind. Soon, half of albums will be bought by people who have passed their 40th birthday.[12]

It is not only in the sphere of recorded music that aging music audiences have been comprehensively targeted. The continuing demand among baby boomers, and post-boomers, to see their generational icons perform live has provided the impetus for a variety of comeback tours and special one-off performances by artists who first rose to prominence in the 1960s and early 1970s—among them, the Who, Steely Dan, and the Eagles. Similarly, British rock group Queen, whose career was brought dramatically to a halt in 1991 with the AIDS-related death of lead singer Freddie Mercury, regrouped in 2005. In that year original members Brian May and Roger Taylor were joined by former Free and Bad Company vocalist Paul Rodgers for what was initially intended as a series of low-key performances

---

12. De Lisle, Melody maker.

but became a forty-two-date world tour (Blake 2008: 95). More recently, in December 2007, legendary seventies rock group Led Zeppelin played a one-off reunion concert at London's O2 Arena, with surviving members Robert Plant, Jimmy Page, and John Paul Jones augmented on stage by drummer Jason Bonham (son of Led Zeppelin's original drummer John Bonham, who died in 1980). The reunion spectacle is not merely limited to rock but is also seen in the sphere of punk and new wave. In 1996, British punk group the Sex Pistols reformed (with original bass player Glen Matlock) for what was to be the first of a string of reunion performances). More recently, original members of The Jam, Bruce Foxton and Rick Buckler, have played a series of concerts under the name From The Jam, while in 2007 the Police re-formed and undertook an extensive world tour.

The ever-expanding tribute band market also offers potent opportunities for aging audiences to relive the live experience of rock groups from their generation who now either are defunct or tour infrequently. An inherently postmodern concept, the tribute band performance plays with time and history, reanimating the voices and images of celebrated and, in many cases deceased, rock icons such as John Lennon, Brian Jones, and Jim Morrison (see Bennett 2006a). In a similar vein, the comeback tours of classic rock and pop artists from the late 1960s and early 1970s have seen an unabashed reliance on the art of self-tribute—certain groups choosing to focus on the live performance of particular albums and songs from their back catalog of recordings because of the demonstrated appeal of this music for a largely middle-aged audience of die-hard fans. For example, the U.S. hard rock group Kiss, under the direction of original group members Gene Simmons and Paul Stanley, recently revived its classic 1970s repertoire and stage image, complete with elaborate face makeup and costumes as well as impressive pyrotechnic displays. The revival was an attempt to re-create, and thus recapture, what many members of the Kiss audience consider to be the most innovative and spectacular period of the group's career. Taking this concept a step further, British heavy metal group Iron Maiden, which first rose to prominence in the early 1980s as part of the New Wave of British Heavy Metal (NWOBHM) (see Bennett 2007), announced in late 2007 its ambitious "Somewhere Back in Time" 2008 world tour. To transport the group, a specially converted Boeing 757 jet airliner was piloted by the group's lead vocalist Bruce Dickinson, a qualified airline pilot. As an accompanying press release explained, "This tour . . . will revisit the band's history by focusing almost entirely on the 80's [sic] in both choice of songs played and the stage set, which will be based around the legendary Egyptian Production of the 1984–85 'Powerslave Tour.'"[13]

Classic rock and pop music has also been extensively featured in television advertisements for goods and services, such as cars, designer-label garments, insurance policies, and credit cards, aimed at an older, more affluent audience. A particularly ambitious example of this is seen in the "Easy Driver" commercial commissioned by the Ford Motor Company in 1999 to promote its then new Ford Cougar model. Directed by Paul Street, this commercial features film actor Dennis Hopper, who first rose to prominence, together with co-star Peter Fonda, in *Easy Rider*, the 1969 counterculture road movie that Hopper also directed (see Denisoff and Romanowski 1991). In an imaginative marketing strategy, Hopper is cast in the commercial as the Ford Cougar driver. Transformed into an affluent-looking, middle-aged professional, sporting short-cropped, graying hair and an immaculate suit, Hopper is seen walking across the dusty forecourt of a remote desert truck stop when he suddenly casts his eyes on a parked chopperized motorcycle identical to the one he rode in *Easy Rider*. Parodying the beginning of the film, Hopper gets into his car and takes to the road to the soundtrack of the Steppenwolf song "Born to Be Wild" (made famous through its use in the opening sequence of *Easy Rider*). Through state-of-the-art digital editing, the present-day Hopper is joined on the road by Billy, the character he portrays in *Easy Rider*, on his chopperized Harley-Davidson. The two are pictured traveling side by side on the open road, mimicking the way Billy and Wyatt (the character played by Peter Fonda) rode together on their motorcycles thirty years earlier in *Easy Rider* (an effect achieved by inserting the present-day Hopper in the Cougar car into original film footage from *Easy Rider* over the image of Fonda, who is edited out of the sequence altogether). The semiotic intentions of the "Easy

---

13. Iron Maiden Official Fansite. Available at http://www.ironmaiden.com/index.php?categoryid=8&p2_articleid=664 (accessed December 31, 2007).

Driver" commercial are not difficult to decipher. The Ford Cougar, an expensive consumer item, is slickly promoted using a series of carefully selected cultural referents designed to appeal to the target market—affluent, middle-aged professionals who came of age during the late 1960s and early 1970s.

Growing Up, Selling Out?

Some observers have suggested that the (re)commodification of baby boomers, their lifestyles, and their musics in the ways described previously simply underscores their status as cultural "tourists"—old, in the way, and nostalgically yearning for their youth. Thus, according to Frith, television commercials that utilize rock classics merely serve to promote "old rock values—brash individualism [and] youthful rebellion . . . as memories and longings that can only be reached by spending money on other goods" (1990: 90). There is, however, a danger here of essentializing the meaning of such texts and the ways in which they are read and understood by aging music fans. Indeed, there is in Frith's argument a clear correspondence with the work of Goldman (1992), for whom television advertisements function in accordance with a logic of late capitalism in which decentered individual subjects are made to fetishize seductively presented consumer objects and images as pathways to contentedness. As more recent work has suggested, however, such is the play of images now prevalent in advertising that audiences may read into them a variety of meanings that do not necessarily correspond with the meanings intended by those who produce them (see, for example, Strinati 1995; O'Donnell 2000). Such "postmodern" studies of advertising adhere to an understanding of audiences not as a passive mass but as active agents in the creation of textual meanings (Fiske 1989; Ang 1996).

A further problem with Frith's reading of the use of "classic" rock tracks in television advertisements is its tendency to categorize baby boomers as a relatively homogeneous socioeconomic group. Obviously, it would be difficult to deny that the spending power associated with the baby-boomer generation has endeared them to the music and other popular cultural industries. That said, it is equally true that not all members of the baby-boomer generation are affluent and thus able, or inclined, to take advantage of the lifestyle products that are advertised through the use of music on television and through associated outlets such as *Mojo* magazine (which invariably comes with a variety of leaflets and flyers for other products, such as CDs, personal stereos, books, and designer-label clothes). Moreover, even in the case of those older fans with the economic capital available to purchase and enjoy lifestyle products such as these, is it really true that such trends in the consumption patterns of baby boomers can be straightforwardly linked to nostalgia? It may be that the use of classic tracks in television commercials is calculated to produce the kinds of nostalgia-induced consumption that Frith and others (see, for example, Savage 1990) refer to. But is this the only, or indeed most important, effect that is actually produced? Do older music fans really think that by spending their money on consumer products they can reclaim their youth—and does this even matter to them? But, most important, are there perhaps other ways of understanding the relationship between aging, music, and identity that are not linked to nostalgia and nostalgic consumption but rather relate to the here and now—to aging music fans' aspirations for the present? Similarly, is it fair to assume that simply because people are beyond the category of youth they are no longer capable of using music in creative, resistant, and political ways? These are clearly significant questions, and ones that have thus far remained unanswered in accounts of aging popular music audiences.

Living in the Past?

Popular music's evocation of time—and time passing—is often cited as one of its most appealing features in the context of everyday listening. As DeNora (2000) notes, individuals are often drawn to particular songs because of the personal or, in certain cases, shared feelings of nostalgia that become attached to them. Songs become imprinted with special memories to such an extent that each time a particular song is heard it replays a series of mental snapshots of the time and/or place that it has come to represent in the mind of the individual listener. Thus, as Kotarba observes: "Invoking a musical style . . . eliminates the need to know dates, years and other precise time markers"

(2002: 401). All of this undoubtedly goes some way toward explaining the continuing importance of music in the lives of older fans. Having invested a great deal of time in listening to music, going to concerts, collecting CDs and records, reading magazines, and perhaps even taking the time to master a musical instrument, these fans may experience music as an important part of their biographical development and, thus, personal history. In this way music can also become a key aspect of the way in which individuals both understand themselves and present themselves to others. For example, in the summer of 1985 I undertook a car journey of several hours to see the newly re-formed British rock band Deep Purple's comeback performance at the Knebworth Festival in England. Among my traveling companions was a man in his late thirties who entertained those in the car with personal recollections of legendary rock performances at which he had been present, notably Jimi Hendrix's appearance at the 1970 Isle of Wight Festival only eighteen days before his death following a drug overdose (see Redding and Appleby 1990). Equally compelling were the man's stories about acquiring records, bootlegs, and various bits of memorabilia, and the sheer depth of his knowledge about the history of heavy rock, blues rock, psychedelia, and the artists associated with each of these genres.

Such personal portraits of life and music are commonplace, and they begin to demonstrate the importance of music in individual life-worlds (see, for example, Cavicchi 1998). Significantly, however, for die-hard fans such as the one described previously, music is about not only where they have been but also where they are going. For this man, music was certainly an important part of his past, but it was also a crucial part of his present and, one might assume, his future. Music had become an integral part of this person's lifestyle to the extent that his life essentially revolved around it. His home was minimally furnished, allowing maximum space for records, videos, and music memorabilia. His job involved working shifts, which enabled scope for traveling to concerts some distance away from his home and attending many of the annual summer festivals in Britain and occasionally elsewhere in Europe. His social milieu principally comprised like-minded individuals—and, perhaps most importantly, his partner shared a commitment to his lifestyle.

Certain aspects of the preceding account accord with DeNora's contention that the nostalgic function of songs can also empower individuals for everyday life in the present by providing a reference point for biographical developments from the past to the present, and from the present into the future. Thus, as DeNora observes:

> Reliving experience through music . . . , in so far as it is experienced as an identification with or of "the past," is part of the work of producing oneself as a coherent being over time, part of producing a retrospection that is in turn a projection into the future, a cuing in how to proceed. In this sense, the past, musically conjured, is a reflexive movement from present to future, the moment-to-moment production of agency in real time. It serves also as a means of putting actors in touch with capacities, reminding them of their accomplished identities, which in turn fuels the ongoing projection of identity from past into future. Musically fostered memories thus produce past trajectories that contain momentum. (2000: 66)

DeNora's observations are instructive in relation to our understanding of the ongoing significance of music for the aging fan. The conceptualization of music as a device that facilitates a perception of the past, present, and future as linked by a process of continuing personal reflection and development provides a basis for exploring long-term investment in a particular popular music genre (or genres) not as social pathology, as writers such as Ross (1994) and Weinstein (2000) suggest, but as a "normal" and increasingly prevalent aspect of the late modern life course in contemporary Western societies.

Forever Young?

This leads on to our second question. What are the sociocultural motivations underlying the long-term investment in popular music and its frequent incorporation into an ongoing lifestyle project? Earlier in this chapter it was noted how journalists and the media have often associated such tendencies with a refusal to grow up and "act one's age." Such attitudes were subsequently challenged on the grounds that they espouse essentialist notions of age that are decidedly out of step with a late modern cultural context in which attitudes toward aging and the life course are rapidly changing. Still, however, there remains a question about what all of this ultimately means for the positioning of the aging popular music fan in relation to a cultural territory that has hitherto been squarely regarded as the domain of youth. How does the increasingly multigenerational nature of audiences for once stridently demarcated "youth" musics such as rock, metal, and punk affect our understanding of these musics and their cultural significance? Indeed, is the concept of youth culture in this context still a valid analytical framework, or should it be abandoned in favor of an alternative concept that encompasses the different age groupings that now associate with rock, metal, punk, and, increasingly, newer genres such as house, techno, and trance? In relation to this it should, of course, be noted that the generational blurring of musical tastes is not a one-way flow, as increasing numbers of young people actively buy into the retro-music market established to cater to the tastes of aging popular music audiences (Hayes 2006; Bennett 2008a). Have we then truly come to a point at which age is simply irrelevant—where boundaries between youth and adulthood have become blurred to the extent that they are no longer visible or, indeed, culturally relevant?

In addressing this question, I find three points noteworthy. First, despite the increasingly multigenerational nature of audiences for some musics, there is a continuing progression of new genres and subgenres that are primarily marketed to, consumed by, and ultimately understood by the young. For example, hard-core and extreme metal are essentially "youth" musics as opposed to musics that are also enjoyed by the majority of middle-aged rock fans—who often claim to find these musics too aggressive and "unmusical" for their tastes (as evidenced in some of the forthcoming accounts of aging music fans in Part II of this book). It seems clear then that the attraction to and appeal of new or emergent styles in rock and pop music are as age-related as they have ever been.

Second, even among those popular music genres whose audiences are becoming more multigenerational, there remain notable differences in the way that fans of different ages respond to the music at both individual and collective levels. For example, Fonarow (1997) notes how the spatial organization of alternative and punk venues tends to be age-related, with younger fans dominating the area directly in front of the stage and the older clientele remaining at the back of the venue, farthest from the stage. Parallel examples of such age-related spatial organization in venue spaces, together with some considerable variations between generations in perceptions of acceptable crowd behavior, were evident in the research conducted for this study (see Chapter 5). Thus, even as certain distinctions between young and old appear to be dissolving in relation to cultural responses to popular music, age and longevity of membership within a particular scene appear to supply a license for specific forms of behavior among older members.

Third, in addressing the phenomenon of the aging music fan, there is a danger of overemphasizing a preoccupation with youthfulness among aging baby boomers and post-boomers. While for some the fact of bodily aging may indeed prompt a reactive drive toward an attempt to remain physically young—for example, through rigorous exercise, body modification, or a simple equation of dressing and acting young with actually *being* young—for many others their perception may be to simply engage in daily activities, hobbies, and interests that have become *natural* for them—and an essential part of who they feel they are rather than who they would "like" to be. Certainly, none of the aging music fans interviewed for this book expressed a desire to be "young" again, and in many cases they were keen to point out the differences they identified between themselves and younger members of the scenes in which they continued to participate. Indeed, a common distinction identified by aging fans between themselves and younger fans centered on a discourse of personal development linked to the aging process. In articulating this discourse, aging fans were concerned to point out that although their identities as hippies, rockers, punks, and so on may have initially taken form in their youth, these identities have continued to develop over the years. In relation to this last point, a number of aging fans interviewed stated that growing older has had advantages in that maturity has prompted them to reevaluate their original youth cultural identities. For some, this reevaluation involved a quite literal process of "dressing down" because they no longer considered the visual image of their teen and twenty-something years to be important to their identity (see Chapter 3). Others stated that the process of growing older has been accompanied by a critical awareness of what they now perceive as the shortcomings and naïveté inherent in their outlook as teenagers and young adults (see Chapter 6).

Music, Aging, and Gender

An inevitable question posed by the research informing this book is the extent to which an ongoing interest in popular music among aging individuals is gender defined. As noted, media stereotypes of aging music fans almost always depict the latter as middle-aged males. Such stereotypes also extend to the realm of popular culture, where portrayals of obsessive, aging male music fans have become almost a cliché. Recent films such as *School of Rock* and the screen adaptation of Nick Hornby's 1995 novel *High Fidelity* are obvious examples of this tendency. The trend toward heavier male investment in music among aging audiences was also evident in the research underpinning this book. For example, during an interview with John, a fifty-five-year-old English hippie, I asked whether he knew of aging female fans who shared his musical tastes or were equally invested in music. John responded, "Well, women move on, don't they?" When I asked John to elaborate on this observation, he offered the opinion that older women "move in different cultural circles," where music is not valued in the same way. John then went on to state that, in his view, older women are generally less interested in music than are older men: "I mean, it's not a talking point in the same way, is it? Y'know, when you talk music in the pub, it's always blokes. An' like, when you go round and see friends, it's always the bloke who gets the old records out, y'know, 'Hey, d'ya remember this?' sort of thing."

In academic research on popular music, the perceived male-centric bias in music consumption—and production—has been linked with other forms of social behavior in which patriarchal discourses and practices of female exscription—defined by Walser (1993: 10) as the "total denial of gender anxieties through the articulation of fantastic worlds without women"—are ingrained. In his ethnographic study of an early 1970s British motorbike gang, Willis draws analogies between the visual image of the biker and basic assumptions concerning male identity as these inform working-class culture. According to Willis, the motorbike itself embodies a "homological" significance that transforms it from a simple mode of transport into a symbol for male courage and camaraderie:

> The solidity, responsiveness, inevitableness [sic], the *strength* of the motor-bike matched the concrete, secure nature of the bikeboys' world. . . . [Its] roughness and intimidation . . . the surprise of its fierce acceleration, the aggressive thumping of the unbaffled exhaust, matches and symbolizes the masculine assertiveness, the rough camaraderie . . . of [the gang's] style of social interaction. (1978: 53)

Willis's observations correspond with other accounts of youth cultures from the late 1960s and early 1970s that similarly point to a strong male bias (see, for example, Hall and Jefferson 1976). Critiques of this work, most notably that of McRobbie (1990), have argued that the male-centric picture of youth cultures created in academic work was matched by a male-centricity in the field of youth research and a consequent emphasis on the male aspects of youth cultural activity. Taking issue with this approach, McRobbie argues that youth cultural groups were by no means "exclusively" male, citing the existence of teddy girls, modettes, and female punks (who applied their own stylistic shock-tactics through spectacular assemblages of female fashion garments) as clear evidence of this. Similarly, McRobbie and Garber (1976) identified a teenybopper culture among teenage girls that, although confined to the domestic space of the bedroom (identified by McRobbie and Garber as a primary space in which teenage girls listen to and talk about music, exchange posters of pop idols, read music-related magazines, and so on), was argued to constitute a form of subcultural activity in itself. Problematically, however, few of the claims made by youth culture researchers in the 1970s are backed up by empirical evidence—and this also extends to female involvement in youth cultural groups. As such, even if we are to acknowledge the existence of female members in youth cultural groups, it is difficult to judge what, if any, qualitative differences existed between male and female youth culturalists in terms of their attitudes toward music, style, and attendant forms of cultural politics.

However, empirically informed research on popular music outside the field of youth culture has similarly pointed to ingrained practices of intolerance toward and exclusion of women in spheres of popular music production, performance, and consumption. Such findings suggest that, irrespective of whether gender influences the actual understanding and use of music in everyday life, opportunities for collective, public engagement with music are delimited according to proscribed gender-determined roles. For example, in her mapping of local music-making practices in Liverpool, Cohen (1991) notes how the absence of women from this scene related to a long-established working-class tradition of patriarchy that infused the local music scene and resulted in a distrust of women, who were considered a threat to the stability of a band. Bayton (1990) adds to this picture of female exclusion by demonstrating how it directly impacts on the physical opportunities for women to become involved in music-making activities. Moreover, as Frith and McRobbie (1990) and Negus (1992) illustrate, such female exclusion is not restricted to local music-making arrangements but also permeates the music industry at all levels, from creative decisions to organizational issues. In terms of music consumption too, research suggests that males vastly outnumber females in pursuits such as record collecting (Straw 1997; Hayes 2006) and attending musical instrument exhibitions and auctions (Ryan and Peterson 2001).

To a degree, such observations pertaining to the gender bias in musical involvement are supported by the findings of this study. Certainly, in conducting the research, I found it difficult to locate older female music fans willing to be interviewed. Moreover, for the most part, those women who did agree to participate in the research wondered why anybody, let alone a white, male academic music researcher, would be interested in what they had to say about music and its importance in their lives. Vroomen has suggested that the sheer prevalence of men in popular music–related activities and the subsequent marking of those activities as a male-dominated territory have, in turn, propagated the view "that mature women are indifferent to popular music and [fostered] the association of women fans with passivity or bad taste" (2004: 245). Indeed, reflecting on my own role in the research process as a male researcher, music fan, and musician, I found that female research participants often assumed that I was more knowledgeable than they were about music and was thus inclined to take their expressed views and opinions less than seriously. While such apprehension could be dispelled to some extent by explaining the purpose of the research, it nevertheless points to a problem inherent in male researchers' seeking female research participants for work of this kind.

Another issue that may well have impacted on the research in relation to the gender balance of participants was a difference in patterns of music consumption among men and women. Several women interviewees said that they felt uncomfortable visiting clubs, venues, and other music-related public forums such as fan conventions, and preferred instead to consume music at home, either alone or in the company of a partner. Again, this corresponds with the findings of Vroomen, whose respondents claimed that their music consumption practices primarily took the form of private home-listening. Moreover, as Vroomen observes, several of her interviewees reported that they reserved listening to their own music as a personal pleasure—something they did only when alone. In addition, Vroomen notes how women also shied away from the more recently available forms of "virtual" engagement with fan bases for particular artists and genres (see, for example, Kibby 2000; Bennett 2002, 2004b; Lee and Peterson 2004), claiming that this practice didn't particularly interest them.

Acquisition of musical taste, relative to age, was also on occasion a point of distinction between male and female interviewees. Thus, while male interviewees generally associated a period of intense teen investment in a particular genre (or genres) of music as a basis for their continuing attachment to music and its attendant cultural sensibilities, female interviewees were less uniform in their accounts as to where their musical tastes had been acquired. For example, Sarah, a forty-four-year-old fan of electronic dance music, claimed never to have really listened to that style of music until she was in her late thirties, when she had been introduced to the dance club scene by male friends. Similarly, Rachel, an interviewee in her mid-thirties, noted that throughout her childhood and early teens she had primarily listened to classical music, this being the musical taste of her parents. According to Rachel, her taste in music only began to change when she left home and went to university. At that point, explained Rachel, she began to listen to a wide variety of music, only settling on preferences for particular artists and genres much later. Interestingly, both Sarah and Rachel were far less fixated on particular notions of musical canon and attendant notions of genre boundary than many of the male fans I interviewed. Rather, their musical tastes were articulated in terms of the aesthetic experience, and general ambience, that particular musics brought to those places in which they spent their leisure time—typically, the home environment. As Rachel put it: "It usually relates to a chord sequence or part of a track . . . if there's a chord sequence I really like. I must be dreadful to live with actually [laughs] because I'll put on a track that I like and I'll repeat it ten times in a row." Such expressed feelings about music also appeared to make female interviewees less inclined to talk about their musical tastes; the deeper, often introspective experiences that older female fans gained through listening to music seemed to be very personal and difficult to articulate.

Location also played some part in determining accessibility to older female fans of popular music. For example, in the case of interviews conducted with aging punks, finding female interviewees in provincial locations proved far more difficult than in urban settings. In the East Kent region of the United Kingdom, where some of the research on aging punks was conducted, the aging punk scene was predominantly male. None of the aging punks interviewed was married to or lived with aging female punks, nor were wives or partners present at the gigs I attended. When asked about their absence, interviewees simply claimed that their wives or partners had no interest in punk music as such. When questioned on the issue of gender among aging punk fans, many interviewees said that other aging punk fans they personally knew tended to be male. On one occasion, Stu, an aging male punk in his late forties, offered to arrange a meeting with an aging female punk friend, but this encounter never transpired. Similarly, my repeated attempts to secure an interview with Jess, an aging female punk recommended by another research respondent, were also unsuccessful. A different situation prevailed in urban settings, where aging female punks were more openly involved in the local scene. In such settings, aging female punks were also more comfortable about being interviewed for the research, as evidenced by my work in Adelaide, South Australia, where I obtained a more gender-balanced interview cohort.

The purpose of this chapter has been to contextualize the aging popular music audience and consider some of the key sociocultural trends informing the significance of music in the articulation and representation of aging identities. As the chapter has illustrated, the phenomenon of the aging popular music fan cannot be reduced to essentialist arguments concerning the arrested development (Calcutt 1998) of adult generations in the wake of the 1950s popular culture boom (see also Riesman [1950] 2001). Nor can the cultural presence of aging popular music fans be explained through a model of economic reductionism that cites the commodification of baby-boomer and post-boomer music tastes—and the resultant "nostalgia" market—as key underpinnings of an aging popular music audience personified in the specter of the "old hippie" or "fifty quid man." Rather, aging popular music audiences must be situated within a broader late modern context of Western societies, where attitudes toward aging and the life course are radically changing. As has been illustrated, one significant facet of this shift has been the centrality of the media and cultural industries in communicating new, positive images of aging and providing resources for the framing of lifestyle projects that stretch across the life course. Aging popular music fans can thus be seen to denote one particular aspect of this new social trend, whereby stylized, aesthetic, and political affiliations with popular music—once rigidly demarcated as the cultural territory of youth—now bespeak the cultural sensibilities of a much broader population demographic.

The following chapter examines the individual and collective life-worlds of aging music fans in order to examines in depth the ways in which music, aging, and biographical development intersect.

2 / Individual and Collective Lifestyles of Aging Popular Music Audiences

Chapter 1 began the task of mapping the social and cultural terrains of the aging baby-boomer and post-boomer generations in the context of late modernity. In this chapter, I discuss the aging music audiences themselves—or, more specifically, their role as active agents, reflexively producing their aging identities through everyday engagement with popular music and its attendant cultural resources. Key to this analysis is the concept of lifestyle, a term associated in a contemporary sense with the cultural turn in sociology (Chaney 1994) and cognate disciplines concerned with the study of culture. As briefly outlined in Chapter 1, integral to the cultural turn is a reinterpretation of culture not purely as a product of socioeconomic forces, but rather as a reflexive *process* encapsulating elements of such forces. Such a view considers the significance of the cultural product within a framework of lifestyle projects constructed by active agents through everyday practices of cultural consumption (Chaney 1996; Bennett 2005). Early forays into the field of cultural consumption as a reflexive process inscribed it with a rhetoric of resistance and opposition to a dominant mainstream culture (see, for example, Fiske 1989). Subsequent work, however, has been more invested in the idea of plotting cultural consumption not merely as a space for directly oppositional practices and strategies but rather as a resource for increasingly rich and diverse articulations of identity within a cultural context that is seen as becoming more pluralistic and fragmented (Chaney 2002).

Building on the contextual frames of reference introduced in Chapter 1, this chapter considers how we might begin to interpret the relationship between popular music, aging, and identity by invoking questions of "value," "authenticity," and "transcendence" as these coalesce around individual and collective lifestyle practices. Again, some measure of qualification is necessary here. The analysis presented in this chapter can, by its very nature, only be extended to those social contexts in which media and cultural consumption have provided a basis for everyday experience and identity formation and practice during the period under investigation—the early 1950s through to the present day. No claims are made in this chapter, or in the subsequent empirical chapters that form Part II of this book, as to how popular music acts as a cultural resource outside Western social settings. There is clearly a need for work that investigates the relationship between popular music and aging in non-Western social and cultural contexts. This investigation, however, is not the aim of this book and is well beyond its scope.

Popular Music, Identity, and Aging

This chapter addresses the critical question of what specifically makes popular music worthy of sustained attention in relation to issues of aging, identity, and lifestyle. Music is, after all, but one form of popular culture produced and consumed in the context of late modernity. Indeed, and as has already been noted in Chapter 1, film, television, and literature also command their own aging audiences; as such, the industries associated with each of these forms of entertainment have advanced considerably toward creating products that cater specifically to older consumers (see Blaikie 1999). Ostensibly then, one could just as easily write about film, television, literature, or a range of other popular cultural products and their impact on the lifestyles and identities of aging individuals. That said, however, in terms of the manner in which it is received and appropriated, music is arguably different from other forms of popular culture in significant ways, not the least of which is in relation to the highly personal connections that individuals form with particular popular music texts and artists. Studies focusing on issues of aesthetics, taste, and textual ownership regarding popular music have been quick to point out the specific kind of relationship that exists between popular music and the audience as compared with other popular cultural forms. A pertinent example here is the work of Frith, which argues that there is

> something specific to musical experience, namely, its direct emotional intensity. Because of its qualities of abstractness (which "serious" aestheticians have always stressed) music is an individualizing form. We absorb songs into our own lives and rhythms into our own bodies; they have a looseness of reference that makes them immediately accessible. Pop songs are open to appropriation for personal use in a way that other popular cultural forms (television soap operas, for example) are not—the latter are tied into meanings we may reject. (1987: 139)

As Frith's observations suggest, embedded in the music-audience relationship are issues of appropriation and identification that are not strictly applicable to other popular cultural forms. This in turn has significant implications for the way in which individuals actively "use" popular music as a resource in their everyday lives. Because music possesses qualities of abstractness, it is also highly malleable; textual meanings can be drawn from music and lyrics in highly subjective and individualized ways. This malleability also engenders strong feelings of textual ownership in relation to popular music. As Frith notes:

> It seems of greater importance to people what they like musically than whether or not they enjoyed a film or television program. . . . [Individuals own] their favorite music in ways that [are] intense and important to them . . . mak[ing] it part of [their] identity and build[ing] it into [their] sense of [them] selves. (Frith 1987: 140, 143)

In this respect it could be argued that theories of popular music that seek to homologize (Willis 1978) its impact on the experience of individual listeners ultimately produce a skewed account of how music works at the individual level.[1] Even if elements of commonality can be deduced among individual consumers of a particular musical style, there is a limit to which this could be described as a "collective" or "group" response to music; individual accounts engaging with the "whyness" of musical taste will ultimately demonstrate more nuanced and personal interpretations of music and its meaning. This was evident in my earlier ethnographic study of local hip-hop scenes in Newcastle upon Tyne, United Kingdom, and Frankfurt am Main, Germany. During the course of this research, interviews with individual members of these respective scenes revealed that the meanings they read into and off rap music and hip-hop culture were far less homogeneous than has often been assumed in subcultural theory and related approaches to understanding the sociocultural significance of popular music (see Bennett 2000).

The tendency of homological explanations of taste-related cultural practice to close off more nuanced understandings of individual reception and appropriation of popular culture resources has long been a point of contention in academic research on audiences. For example, in considering the contribution of fan studies to our understanding of popular culture's everyday meanings, Bloustien suggests that fan studies "serve to remind us that [audiences] may not be as bounded, homogenous, spontaneous, and class-based or even as age-based as many analytical constructs suggest" (2004a: 149). A study that bears out Bloustien's observations is Cavicchi's *Tramps Like Us* (1998), an empirical examination of the fan base for U.S. rock icon Bruce Springsteen. As Cavicchi notes, in conducting the study, he intended to peer into the lifeworlds of individual Springsteen fans in order to create an ethnographically rich description (Geertz 1973) of what attracts them to the music of Springsteen. Similarly, Cavicchi was concerned

---

1. Indeed, this has become a key criticism of Willis's work (1978) on the homological relationship between musical taste, style, and class background in the case of biker and hippie cultures (see Cohen 1987; Bennett 2008b).

to discover how these fans made use of Springsteen's music in their everyday lives. There is certainly a value in Cavicchi's approach, not least in its creation of what could be referred to as a "folk model" (Jenkins 1983) of popular music fandom. This folk model offers a refreshing alternative to the top-down, theory-driven analyses often applied in the study of popular music audiences. Moreover, Cavicchi's work provides an important insight regarding the capacity of popular music, in this case supported by the iconic status of Springsteen as a "working-class hero," to engage at a personal level with the lifeworlds of individual music fans—their aesthetic sensibilities, lifestyle preferences, perceptions of themselves, and their place within their particular local environments. In this way, Cavicchi's work takes some important steps toward situating the cultural significance of popular music within the mundane, everyday contexts where it is consumed and interpreted as a cultural text. This approach also sets out some important parameters for studying popular music's appeal at the everyday level, and its significance in "provid[ing] an experience that transcends the mundane, that takes us 'out of ourselves'" (Frith 1987: 144). Again, with some few exceptions,[2] research that has focused on this aspect of popular music's cultural significance has been heavily invested in youth culture. Indeed, Frith, whose work offers highly instructive insights into the aestheticization of popular music at an everyday level, has himself suggested that "people's heaviest investment in popular music is when they are teenagers and young adults. . . . People do use music less, and less intently, as they grow up" (1987: 143).

Whether or not one subscribes to Frith's assessment of individuals' everyday investments in popular music as a cultural resource, there can be no doubt that it is a perception that has weighed heavily on the direction of popular music scholarship since its inception in the late 1970s. Moreover, in research venturing into the realm of popular music consumption, in which discussion of the shifting age demographic of popular music audiences could feasibly have been facilitated, writers have tended instead to concern themselves with *mediums* for the consumption of popular music rather than with the

---

2. See, for example, DeNora (2004) and Bennett (2006a).

audience per se. Examples here include live performance (Kotarba 1994), cinema (Smith 2001), radio (Rothenbuhler and McCourt 1992), and music television (Kaplan 1987). Although undoubtedly an important frame of reference for our understanding of how audiences gain access to popular music, such a medium-centered focus is at the same time arguably too narrow to illustrate the broader spectrum of musical experience as this touches the lives of individuals in an everyday context. Indeed, some evidence now suggests that "music consumption" and "musical experience" are not necessarily synonymous. Thus, for example, as DeNora (2000) observes, how individuals operationalize music in their everyday lives may have no direct cognitive relationship with the actual experience of listening to music in either a live or mechanically reproduced context. Rather, though a medium of music consumption can act as a stimulus, the everyday meaning of the musical text itself is also produced through the way in which the text becomes embedded in the individual subject's consciousness. For example, a song heard on a breakfast radio show may trigger a mood or sensation that remains with the individual throughout the day. Moreover, the subjective application of such embodied texts by individuals may be infinitely diverse; to suggest that individuals use music purely, say, as an escapist strategy to block out mundane, tedious, difficult, and challenging aspects of their lives is to delimit the range of purposes for which music impacts on and informs the strategies and sensibilities employed by individuals in their everyday lives.

The abstraction of musical meaning from the direct experience of listening to music, and attendant notions of music as a purely leisure-based resource, in this way arguably facilitates a rather different understanding of music's role in relation to identity formation and the ontological experience of the self. Again, this may have important and specific implications for how we understand the musical experience of the aging audience. Thus, to return to a key concern of this book, such an interpretation and understanding of musical affect may facilitate an extrapolation of how longevity of individual investment in a certain genre, or genres, of popular music ultimately weaves its own dynamic of musical meaning. Most significantly, music itself may take on a heightened level of importance through an individual's long-standing immersion in musical texts and the ways in which these roll out and intersect with critical points in the life course. To cite the most obvious examples of this, songs with lyrics that are known "inside out" or certain chord or riff sequences present in a favorite song may evoke a particular mood, thus constituting important emotional reference points for aging popular music fans when reflecting on specific aspects or periods of their lives. Embedded in memory and embodied through reflection on their relation to individual biography, popular music can thus become an important source of life-mapping for aging popular music fans. Popular music may also form an important part of reflection—or indeed speculation—about relationships, careers, bringing up children, the actual physical process of getting older, and so on. In each of these and other everyday contexts, the part played by music as a source of inspiration, comfort, assurance, memory, and so on renders it inseparable from the physical and experiential processes associated with growing older. At the same time, and as subsequent chapters in this book seek to illustrate, music can act as a critical driver within and across a number of dimensions of the aging individual's life course, influencing career path, peer and family relations, and political and spiritual outlook into middle age and beyond. In these ways music becomes an integral aspect of individuals' personal history—and an inseparable part of their ontological understanding of their biographical development. This observation is supported by Grossberg, who suggests that while such transgressive qualities of music are most typically associated with youth, "they have long since exceeded that and become implicated in a more historical struggle over the affective organisation of everyday life" (1992: 165). The task thus becomes one of understanding the actual everyday process through which musical affect takes shape and form in the construction and articulation of aging identities.

Popular Music, Lifestyle, and Aging

An important stepping-stone in this process is the reemergence of *lifestyle* within critical thinking about identity and belonging in contemporary social settings. Drawing on Weberian perspectives relating to the formation of status groups within society, contemporary exponents of lifestyle theory such as Reimer (1995), Chaney (1996), and Miles (2000) have applied the concept as a means of examining the ways in which late modern individuals draw upon the cultural resources around them as a means of constructing reflexively articulated identities. In this context, the term "lifestyle" is applied to denote clusters of cultural practices, and attendant aesthetic sensibilities, within which reflexive identities are grounded. Although individually derived, lifestyle projects draw on widely available commodities, images, and texts, thus underscoring common patterns of taste and aesthetic sensibilities. Indeed, individual lifestyles frequently converge to the point where they form the basis for new forms of collective cultural identity in late modern social settings (Bennett 1999). In an attempt to explicate the process of negotiation, affect, and sociality underscoring the production, management, and articulation of late modern lifestyle projects, Chaney sets out a theoretical model based on what he terms lifestyle "sites" and "strategies." According to Chaney, lifestyle *sites* refer to the "physical metaphors for the spaces that actors can appropriate and control," while *strategies* denote the "characteristic modes of social engagement, or narratives of identity, in which the actors concerned can embed the metaphors at hand" (1996: 92). Integral to this application of lifestyle is an understanding of cultural meaning in contemporary society as not fully fashioned and received by social actors in a passive, uncritical way. Rather, argues Chaney, the significance of cultural meaning relates to its status as a reflexive process; through their appropriation and reworking of cultural resources, individuals inscribe them with meanings of their own.

Since its reintroduction into contemporary sociological thinking, lifestyle theory has been frequently criticized as an aspect of what McGuigan (1992) refers to as "cultural populism." Identified with current political trends toward neo-liberalism, lifestyle is regarded as uncritically championing the freedom of the latter-day consumer to freely choose between different identity projects, seemingly oblivious to the structural constraints, notably class, gender, and race, together with other socially ingrained forms of inequality, such as poverty and disability. In truth, however, Chaney's model of lifestyle seeks not to disregard such structural constraints on contemporary social life. Instead, Chaney is concerned with illustrating how lifestyle sites and strategies offer a means for the negotiation of such constraints. Within such processes of negotiation, structural constraints may be symbolically worked over and worked across. A clear illustration of this in a contemporary idiom is hip-hop. The work of theorists such as Gilroy (1993) has interpreted hip-hop as an expression of the global African diaspora and thus linked to particular understandings of ethnic and cultural identity situated in discourses of postcolonialism. However, through its everyday appropriation and reworking in myriad sociocultural contexts, hip-hop has proven itself resilient to such specific forms of theorization. It has become instead a potent, and often highly politicized, form of global youth culture, bridging divides between youth from a diverse range of ethnic and cultural backgrounds dispersed across the globe (Mitchell 1996; Bennett 2000). It is possible to see the appropriation and reworking of popular music and its attendant cultural resources by aging audiences in a broadly similar fashion. Through their ongoing engagement with postwar popular music genres as culturally meaningful, aging audiences have overturned previous connotations of these musics as exclusively youth-centred. In doing so, they have brought new meanings to bear on these musics, which are tied up with the reflexive production of aging identities.

In the consideration of the aestheticization of popular music as a means of constructing and performing aging identities, lifestyle is an important theoretical framing device. Key to its full utilization in this respect is an understanding of the three critical practices—*appropriation, inscription*, and *representation*—through which aging individuals establish and enact individual and shared lifestyle projects.

Appropriation

In all current accounts of lifestyle, the act of appropriation is considered coterminous with the act of consumption. As noted, this rather narrow interpretation of appropriation has been readily seized upon in "cultural populism" critiques, which have been quick to proclaim that late modern lifestyles are open only to those who can afford them; that lifestyles do not denote freely chosen identities at all but are merely symbolic of the economic power on which they are built. Such an interpretation, however, falls short of understanding the broader sphere of everyday life experience through which individuals encounter, absorb, and make use of physical and symbolic cultural resources. Given the often intangible qualities of musical experience and its increasing ubiquitousness in the contemporary mediascape (Appadurai 1990), popular music warrants special attention in this respect. Indeed, the everyday appropriation of popular music can take place at a variety of levels that often involve no direct form of economic exchange. For example, a primary medium through which individuals experience music is radio. As a key interlocutor of popular music in both private and public spaces, radio provides a characteristically wide spectrum of popular music on a daily basis and is relatively easy to access. The increasing fragmentation of radio audiences, now as often marked by generation as by particular genre taste, has resulted in greater specialization of radio to cater to its diversifying audience (Glevarec and Pinet 2008). Similarly, the increasing availability of popular music as downloadable sound files via the Internet has significantly boosted access to music at a relatively low cost (see, for example, Rojek 2005). At a more low-tech level, the frequency of "burning" and exchange of CDs between friends and acquaintances is also a relatively low-cost of way of accessing music. Furthermore, and as noted in Chapter 1, films, television series, and documentaries featuring music and music-related cultural images, texts, and objects from various eras of contemporary popular music history also serve as important resources for aging popular music audiences.

The everyday appropriation of popular music can therefore now take place in a variety of contexts that are not strictly determined by personal wealth and concomitant economic status. Such processes of appropriation as those outlined previously in turn underscore new ways of understanding everyday enactments of appropriation in the context of lifestyle sites and strategies. Thus, rather than always being intended to conspicuously demonstrate wealth and status, appropriation may also denote more emotive, introspective, and intangible forms of everyday engagement with objects, images, and texts produced and disseminated by the cultural industries. Through their emotive positioning of music, as much as through consumption of music on a more conspicuous level, aging individuals forge associations with each other through the similar forms of cultural value they inscribe within particular musical texts and genres.

Inscription

The process of inscription denotes the way in which cultural resources are symbolically reworked to assume new, often highly particularized, forms of meaning within lifestyle projects. Typically, exponents of lifestyle theory have examined the process of inscription in relation to the reworking of commodities (Miles 2000) and the cultural demarcation of physical spaces such as suburbia and the new inner-city bohemia (Chaney 1997). Again, it is often the conspicuous value of cultural resources as visual demarcators of lifestyle sites and strategies that is highlighted in such work. Clearly, this aspect of lifestyle production, management, and articulation has considerable significance for the discussion of aging popular music audiences.

Of equal importance in the forging of aesthetically aligned cultural groupings, however, is the way in which individuals affectively associate themselves with others through their cultural investment in specific products, images, texts, and so on. Although physically enacted performances of common lifestyle association are possible within particular local spaces, of which the suburb and gentrified inner-city zone are obvious examples in contemporary social settings, lifestyle projects that symbolically bond individuals and groups also occur translocally and, indeed, globally (see, for example, Hodkinson 2004; Hodgkinson 2004). At such physical distance from each other, parallel articulations of lifestyle sites and strategies are enacted primarily at the affective level. To focus specifically on the example of popular music, such affective qualities of lifestyle sites and strategies are potently demonstrated through the way in which a successive variety of musical genres, from rock 'n' roll in the 1950s through to more contemporary forms such as rap and dance music, have provided the basis for globally articulated forms of cultural practice (Bennett 2001a). Although enacted in particular local spaces, and thus taking on locally nuanced physical articulations (Bennett 2000), such genres have provided a stock of resources for the construction and articulation of broadly similar lifestyle projects among youth cultural groups spread across the globe.

In relation to popular music, the tenacity of such affective belonging has largely been achieved through the music's openness to practices of symbolic inscription that affectively connect groups across geographical and often sociopolitical divides.[3] Although, as observers such as Frith (1981, 1983) have noted, the conflation of such affective forms of belonging with a concrete sense of "community" has proved little more than a potent myth in the history of postwar popular music, there are, nevertheless, clear indications that affective belonging can and does provide a basis for more physical, albeit temporary, expression of sociality at specific nodal points for translocal gatherings such as festivals (Dowd, Liddle, and Nelson 2004) and dance music events (Carrington and Wilson 2002).

Similarly, in his assessment of the impact of rock music on the culture of late modern society, Grossberg (1984, 1986) suggests that this impact can be most clearly discerned through the affective alliances it has helped to foster among audiences in a global context. The concept of affectivity and belonging among aging audiences is returned to later in this chapter, where it will be argued that affectivity provides an important source of connection and aesthetic bonding for the lifestyle projects of aging popular music fans through the building of what is referred to as affective scenes.

Representation

The representation of cultural goods, images, and texts as a basis for contemporary lifestyles has been fruitfully mapped across sociology (Chaney 1996; Miles 2000), and cultural and media studies (Ang 1996; Lull 1995). The emphasis within such work, however, has been on charting the process and significance of re-representation in relation to specific media, notably television and cinema, and consumer objects rather than on looking at the role of the audience. This emphasis also applies to the emergent research field of aging and popular culture, where again the focus has been squarely on examining mass-produced objects, images, and texts produced for aging audiences (Blaikie 1999) and their function in presenting "positive

---

3. See, for example, Easton's (1989) study of countercultural rock in the Soviet Union.

images of ageing" (Featherstone and Hepworth 1995; see also Chapter 1). By comparison, little has been said about the importance of such objects, images, and texts in the construction of lifestyles among aging audiences.

Clearly, however, there is ample scope in lifestyle theory to consider the role of the audience in the re-representation of cultural images, objects, and texts as part of the process involved in the production, maintenance, and articulation of lifestyles. In the context of aging music audiences, their representation of musical texts and related cultural artifacts through the lens of collective lifestyle sites and strategies throws a critical light on how such texts and artifacts are creatively transformed into highly particularized props for the staging of aging identities. Such identities are organized around the understanding and discursive positioning of artifacts as long-term articulators of a cultural self and the positioning of that self within a particular cultural milieu. The concept of milieu takes on significant resonance here as a means of demarcating certain temporally situated meanings and levels of significance as these coalesce around popular music artifacts. Indeed, and as subsequent chapters in this book illustrate, generationally demarcated popular music audiences often attach as much importance to a particular era in the history of a given genre—for example, rock, punk, rap, or dance—as they do to the music, imagery, and cultural practices associated with such genres.

A replica of an original Woodstock poster framed on the living room wall of an aging baby boomer, or a fifty-year-old heavy rock fan wearing a T-shirt from the original 1980 Castle Donington rock festival, may thus function to articulate not merely a form of musical taste but also a generationally informed lifestyle aesthetic. Through such common, everyday representations of musical meaning, artifacts such as these serve as an important situating strategy for aging music audiences. In this way generational bonds between aging generations of music fans are not only preserved but also managed and remade. Common understandings and experiences of musical texts in turn provide individuals with common understandings and experiences as to how they have aged, not only physically and socially but also *culturally*.

Lifestyle Sites and Strategies in Context

If lifestyle sites and strategies offer a useful conceptual framework for the theorization of aging audiences' production and articulation of identities through their ongoing investment in musical and extra-musical resources, understanding the practical everyday enactment of such sites and strategies is also clearly important. In popular discourse, especially in the media and on the Internet, it has become fashionable to talk about "aging" subcultures and aging subcultural lifestyles.[4] Typically, such observations apply an uncritical perspective that over-looks the theoretical embedment of subculture within a series of sociological and cultural studies-based work on social inequality and patterns of resistance. In this context, subculture has been used as a means of marking off particular groups from a perceived "dominant" or "mainstream" culture, with the distinction between subculture and dominant culture revolving around issues of age and economic power (Bennett 1999).[5] However, given that common musical tastes and associated stylistic preferences are increasingly observed *across* generations, such distinctions are becoming more difficult to main-tain. This fact is illustrated by the many middle-aged professionals who continue to engage in hobbies and interests retained from their youth that could ostensibly be described as subcultural. A pertinent example of this is offered in McDonald-Walker's work on contempo-rary biker culture. As McDonald-Walker observes, it is those "in the 30–59 age range . . . with disposable wealth and company cars, who

---

4. See, for example, the Web site entitled Hippie Roots & The Perennial Subcul-ture. Available at http://www.hippy.com/php/article-243.html (accessed October 22, 2012).

5. For an exception, see Macbeth's (1992) application of subculture to ocean cruis-ers—individuals typically in their thirties or older who give up their day jobs, sell their homes, and become full-time amateur sailors, touring the world in yachts or schooners. Arguably, however, what Macbeth is describing here is not a "sub-culture" as this is conventionally understood in youth research. Rather, Macbeth has taken the term and redeployed it to describe a radically different scenario in which individuals, motivated by a variety of different—and indeterminate—factors, actively choose to adopt an alternative lifestyle.

now constitute the major profile for motorcycling" (1998: 389). Similarly, Ryan and Peterson (2001) note how the market for rare and vintage electric guitar models, originally made popular through their use by sixties rock countercultural icons such as Jimi Hendrix, Eric Clapton, and Pete Townshend, is dominated by middle-aged professional males whose high income allows them to purchase such prized musical instruments. Such examples lend weight to Chaney's (2002, 2004) argument that late modern culture has become *fragmented* to the extent that distinctions between so-called subcultures and dominant cultures are now essentially meaningless. Thus, according to Chaney, "The qualities of appropriation and innovation once applied to subcultures can be seen in relation to a range of consumer and leisure-based groupings across the social spectrum" (2004: 41).

In a body of work now collectively referred to as post-subcultural theory (see, for example, Muggleton 2000; Muggleton and Weinzierl 2003; Bennett and Kahn-Harris 2004; Bennett and Peterson 2004), the concept of *scene* has been put forward as a model more suited to understanding and interpreting collective expressions of lifestyle and taste in late modern societies. Scenes function not because they are tied to preexisting notions of community based on class, tradition, and so on, but because they facilitate new forms of collectivity based on shared participation in more recent forms of material culture. In their application to popular music, scenes have been interpreted as embracing a broad range of activities, including music-making, production, promotion, and consumption—as well as the necessary infrastructure of physical resources, such as venues, clubs, rehearsal spaces, recording studios, and record and music shops, needed to sustain such activities (Stahl 2004). A further aspect of scenes that gives them a distinctly late modern character of reflexivity is the multiplicity of spaces in which scene activity takes place. Thus, according to Straw, scenes often transcend particular localities "reflect[ing] and actualiz[ing] a particular state of relations between various populations and social groups, as these coalesce around particular coalitions of musical style" (1991: 379).

More recent work has developed Straw's notion of music scenes as multiply articulated, transgressive phenomena. Important in this respect is Peterson and Bennett's (2004) introduction of a three-tier model of music scenes. This comprises the already familiar terms "local" and "translocal" scene and adds a new category in the form of "virtual" scene. As this term suggests, virtual scenes utilize Internet communication technology, thus allowing geographically dispersed fans to interact online. As Peterson and Bennett observe:

> Whereas a conventional local scene is kept in motion by a series of gigs, club nights, fairs, and similar events, where fans converge, communicate and reinforce their sense of belonging to a particular scene, the virtual scene involves direct Net-mediated person-to-person communication between fans. . . . This may involve, for example, the creation of chat-rooms or list-servs dedicated to the scene and may involve the trading of music and images online. (2004: 11)

The notion of the virtual scene thus opens up a new means of conceptualizing scene membership, not necessarily as a face-to-face activity but as something that is enacted primarily, if not exclusively, through the virtual spaces of the Internet. In this way the Internet becomes an important new medium for forms of musicalized association, with the physical, face-to-face forms of interaction that characterize the local scene being replaced by new forms of interaction that center primarily on articulations of knowledge, taste, and authority that accompany a prolonged commitment to a particular genre or genres of music.

In their original conceptualization of music scenes, Peterson and Bennett align certain qualities—"local," "translocal," and "virtual"— with case studies of specific scenes. However, it follows that no one music scene need be exclusively local, translocal, or virtual but may exhibit properties associated with each of these categories. Although not directly addressed by Peterson and Bennett, the rethinking of music scenes in this way also offers new insights into the variety of practices through which aging audiences retain a commitment to their preferred music and is, therefore, particularly useful for our understanding of the lifestyle practices of aging audiences. That the concept of scene bears important theoretical and empirical significance for the study of aging popular music audiences is evident among the personal accounts that I collected from aging audience members and that form the basis for Part II of this book. For example, in Chapters 4 and 5, aging clubbers and punks relate accounts that illustrate the ongoing importance of local, physical scenes for them as a means through which to articulate their individual and collective lifestyle projects and continuing cultural investment in music. In other cases, however, those interviewed claimed that their involvement in physical scenes had become less frequent and/or important for a variety of personally, domestically, and economically motivated reasons. Such a lack of involvement in a local scene, however, was sometimes compensated for through attendance at special events, such as annual festivals and conventions. Such translocal gatherings enable those older fans with less opportunity to engage in regular activity in a local scene to nevertheless maintain a sense of belonging to a scene. Applying this argument with specific reference to festivals, Dowd, Liddle, and Nelson note that

> while music festivals occur more rarely than do events that constitute local scenes, the intensity of a festival compensates for its infrequency. Drawn together from geographically dispersed locations and away from the expectations of everyday life, fans and performers can immerse themselves in [the festival] culture. (2004: 149)

Dowd, Liddle, and Nelson's interpretation of festival spaces as scenes in themselves has a special resonance for our understanding of aging popular music audiences and their ongoing attachment to music and its associated cultural practices. Thus, as a number of those interviewed for this book explained, if their club and pub-going activities had dwindled, this drop-off was compensated for by their attendance at annual festivals, such as WOMAD (see Chapter 5).

Alternatively, aging popular music fans may never meet in face-to-face contexts at all but still involve themselves in music through participation in virtual scenes. As Kibby (2000) and Bennett (2002, 2004b) observe, an added advantage of scene involvement in this way is that it enables geographically isolated individuals, including those with quite specialist musical interests, to form online associations with other fans and participate in the collective life of a scene from the private sphere of their own home. As illustrated in Chapter 4, there is some evidence that aging popular music fans use the Internet to communicate with those of a similar age with shared musical and lifestyle preferences. That said, it is also true to say that the Internet plays less of a role in the lives of aging popular music fans than might have been anticipated. Indeed, some interviewees observed that, beyond buying music or related products such as books online, their interest and ongoing cultural investment in music were not particularly well served by the Internet and the forms of online engagement it affords. Such accounts correspond with Vroomen's study (2004) of older female fans of British pop singer Kate Bush. Several of them claimed to have been discouraged from participating in e-mail lists and chat rooms posted on fan sites because of the obsessive type of fandom they associated with such communication mediums.

As Vroomen's observations help to illustrate, virtual scenes are by no means all-inclusive. On the contrary, like other scenes, they also exhibit exclusionary dimensions. Just as local scenes may demand visual displays of "scene competence"—for example, fashion sense or proficiency in a particular dance style (Thornton 1995)—virtual music scenes require other forms of competence. Detailed knowledge of a specific artist, or an ability—and willingness—to critically evaluate and judge particular songs, albums, and so on, often assumes equal importance as a symbol of status and belonging. The need for such shows of competence often acts as a barrier to participation in virtual scenes and may be off-putting, especially to older fans, who, as Vroomen's work illustrates, may not feel the need to articulate their attachment to a particular genre or artist in such a way. At a more fundamental level, a lack of basic technical competence and/or economic resources may also block individual access to and participation in virtual music scenes. A study by Facer and Furlong is telling in this respect as it reveals how the use of information technology and levels of computer literacy among young people mirror those of their parents and "is patterned along socioeconomic lines" (2001: 459). Indeed, age itself may play a significant role here too, with levels of computer literacy decreasing relative to age.[6]

Affective Scenes

There remains, then, a problem of where to position those aging music fans who do not fit neatly into any of the three scene categories put forward in Peterson and Bennett's (2004) typology. Arguably, a new category, "affective scene," needs to be added to Peterson and Bennett's existing three-tier model of scenes. Clearly, all scenes embrace some level of affectivity, a point effectively made by Shank (1994) in his study of the local music scene in Austin, Texas. In the case of aging audiences, however, especially those whose continuing investment in music is practiced at a more individualized level, a modified reading of the affective scene is arguably called for. Such a scene may express itself through more introspective gestures, such as the retention of a generational mindset whose most physical manifestation comes through the consumption of particular media—for example, retro music magazines such as *Mojo* and *Classic Rock*—or perhaps simply through listening to music in the private sphere of one's home. Aging music audiences may use such mediums to affectively situate themselves within a community of like-minded others.

As with Anderson's (1983) "imagined communities" of newspaper readers in particular national settings, affective scenes are underpinned by a knowingness on the part of isolated individuals that many others are listening to the same music, reading the same music literature, watching the same music-related films and documentaries, and—above all—making a similar sort of sense from what they are hearing, reading, and watching, based upon their shared generational memories and cultural experience of that music. That such affective practices can also provide people with a sense of "sceneness" is again illustrated in Vroomen's study of older female Kate Bush fans. According to Vroomen, although these fans were invisible to each other in

---

6. Obviously, this is set to change in coming decades as those born during the information technology revolution enter middle age.

the sense that they did not "gather or display their fandom publicly," a feeling of sceneness was still evident: "The fact that these women were keen to take part in [my] research and to share their experiences with me—encouraged by our mutual recognition as fans—suggests the possible existence of a scene, albeit a more loosely defined one based on shared feelings and knowledge" (2004: 240).

This notion of a scene, based not on any palpable form of interaction with others but rather organized around "shared feelings and knowledge," seems an important advancement in current thinking about music scenes. In general terms, the concept of music scene is considered, by definition, to be tied to some form of *tangible* collective life, whether manifested at a local, face-to-face level or in translocal or virtual capacities that are more temporal and transient. For Vroomen's respondents, a sense of scene manifested itself primarily through listening to and/or thinking about music (in this case the music of Kate Bush) in an individual capacity. These women simply did not feel a need to engage in conventional instances of fan activity—such as conventions and Internet fan sites. That said, however, they were also clearly aware of themselves as having at some level a commonality derived from a particular kind of experience they shared as individual, "private" listeners to Kate Bush's music.

In the case of Vroomen's work, the affective scene members that she identifies have seemingly always associated with Kate Bush and her music on a home-based, individualized footing. Affective bonds shared by individuals in the present may, however, be grounded in a more physically experienced sense of collectivity that figured in the past—that is to say, in earlier affiliations with youth cultural groups and/or associated scenes and events. For such individuals, their affective sense of belonging is grounded in a memory of having "been there"—for example, a mod in the mid-1960s, a hippie in the late 1960s, a punk in the late 1970s, and so on. Again, there are clear parallels here with Grossberg's (1984, 1986) notion of rock music forging an "affective alliance" among globally dispersed audiences. For these audiences, an initial investment in the physical scenes of rock culture during the late 1960s and early 1970s has remained with them as an affective sense of belonging grounded in a generationally shared understanding of rock's cultural meaning and significance.

Likewise, in important ways the notion of an affective scene accurately befits the experiences of a number of aging music audience members interviewed for this book. Many spoke about earlier involvement in physically enacted, face-to-face music scenes associated with youth cultural groupings and how the memories of them continued to inform their sense of connection with music and its significance in their everyday lives. An analogous, if far more dramatic, expression of affective belonging generated through collective memory in this way is that articulated by the veterans of particular war campaigns. For those individuals, the gravity of such campaigns and the experiential mark they leave can only be properly known and understood by others who were actually there and collectively shared the experience.

Through applying the concept of lifestyle, this chapter has focused on theoretically addressing the everyday processes through which popular music retains significance for aging audiences. Drawing on the work of Chaney (1996), I have argued that the lifestyles of aging music audiences are creative projects that involve the appropriation, inscription, and representation of musical texts and associated cultural resources. It has further been illustrated how the everyday use of music by aging audiences transforms it into a palpable resource in the reflexive production, management, and articulation of aging identities. Popular music's significance in this context, it has been argued, may take a variety of forms. At an individual level, it may offer opportunities for reflection and/or speculation on the biographical development of the aging self. Such a process of reflection and speculation may be enacted with an ongoing sense of affective attachment to a generationally informed cultural milieu. At a collective level, popular music may offer avenues for connection between members of aging audiences as their ongoing investments in music and resulting cultural sensibilities inform lifestyle projects that cluster into collective forms of scene activity.

Part II of this book explores empirically some of the myriad ways in which popular music, intertwined with a variety of other everyday material objects, activities, discourses, and aesthetic sensibilities, assumes such a critical underpinning in relation to aging identities. Each of the four chapters in Part II presents a series of case studies and vignettes focusing on specific aspects of the relationship between popular music and aging in late modernity. Each chapter builds on and develops the themes and issues raised in Chapters 1 and 2 as a means of illustrating their empirical application in investigating the lifestyles constructed by aging audience members around their musical tastes.

II / Case Studies

3 / Toning Down
the Mohawk

Music, Style, and Aging

A characteristically defining feature of popular music genres from the 1950s onward has been the stylistic innovations that have grown up around them. Almost every post–Second World War popular music genre, from rock 'n' roll through hard rock and glam to punk, goth, and hip-hop, has been spectacularly demarcated by the visual style of artists and audiences associated with these musics. The significance of music-based style has been most comprehensively mapped in relation to youth. Beginning with the Birmingham Centre for Contemporary Cultural Studies (CCCS) in the 1970s (see Hall and Jefferson 1976) and continuing in the post-CCCS work of Hebdige (1979), style as a visual appendage of youth "subcultures" was argued to mark out strategies of resistance to an array of social maladies, from class inequality and unemployment (Jefferson 1976) to social exclusion and racism (Chambers 1976). In the 1990s, a new chapter in the analysis of music-based style began with the emergence of post-subcultural theory. Embracing key tenets of postmodernism while simultaneously employing a Weberian model for the interpretation of social status, post-subcultural theory sought to rethink class-based subcultural explanations of style in the face of the alleged individualization and heightened reflexivity ushered in by a new age of consumer choice and lifestyle marketing (Polhemus 1997; Miles 2000; Muggleton 2000).

Up until the early 1980s, the youth-centered credentials of popular music–related styles were relatively easy to qualify in academic writing. Those investing in such styles were primarily "young" people, that is to say, between the ages of sixteen and twenty-five. Over a quarter of a century later, however, the positioning of popular music–related styles as youth centered seems far less productive as an analytical strategy for understanding the significance of these styles as cultural markers of identity. While classic style-based musics such as punk, hard rock, metal, and goth, together with a range of other genres that originated in the 1970s and 1980s, continue to thrive, the scenes now focused on these musics could hardly be described as the exclusive domain of youth; rather, such scenes are essentially multigenerational, their memberships comprising individuals spanning the generations from teenager to fifty- and, in some cases, sixty-something. Consequently, reading punk, rock, metal, and so on as "youth" musics is to ignore their wider significance among a post-youth audience. The same applies to the visual styles associated with these musics. If conventional readings of style continue to associate them primarily with youth culture, the fact is that a much broader age cohort now invests in aspects of style and the aesthetic sensibilities ingrained within them. While in many instances the style projects of older fans may be toned-down versions of their earlier youth images, they are, nonetheless, forms of stylistic association and thus warrant analytical attention.

The "Post-youth" Meaning of Style

One obvious problem here is how to position established theories of style—those that have been applied in the study of youth culture—to individuals now in middle age and, increasingly, approaching later life. For these aging groups of "stylists," discourses of resistance, subversion, or rebellion, at least as these have conventionally been used to talk about the meaning of youth style, have no straightforward application.[1] This is not to suggest that age strips style of any form of subversive meaning. It is all too easy to glibly dismiss the middle-aged, middle-class biker who takes out her motorcycle each Sunday afternoon for a leisurely tour to a country pub with a rock 'n' roll jukebox, or the sixty-year-old hippie with his own design company whose festival-going activities have dwindled to an annual trip to Glastonbury. Certainly, these aging examples of biker and hippie culture are very different, at least in terms of socioeconomic standing, from the young bikers and hippies interviewed by Willis (1978) during the early 1970s. Similarly, the middle-aged punk going down to his local pub for a game of darts, or picking his young daughter up from school, does not correspond in any obvious sense with the Hebdigian version of the young punk using and abusing his or her body as a means of picking fault with the social system (see Hebdige 1979). Yet the very presence of such aging examples of "youth" cultural affiliation suggests a series of questions, as yet unanswered, about the meaning of style in middle age and beyond.

As noted, classic analyses of youth cultural style, notably those produced by the CCCS, have tended to couch their interpretation of style in a Marxist-influenced, stucturalist framework that relates stylistic preference and musical taste directly to class—more specifically, class conflict and hegemonic struggle (see Bennett 1999). A by-product of this has been the reduction of style and its everyday embodiment in what Waters (1981) once referred to as a "half-formed, inarticulate radicalism." By contrast, "post-subcultural" explanations of style put forward by theorists such as Muggleton (2000) and Miles (2000) allow for a greater sense of reflexivity on the part of social actors in their embodiment of style. Again, however, for a number of reasons, post-subcultural theory may be a less than effective framework for understanding the stylistic preferences of aging popular music fans.

As this chapter illustrates, among such fans, a previous emphasis on visual style has often receded in importance, with individual identity politics taking on a far more subtle and nuanced dimension.

---

1. Indeed, it is highly debatable whether such discourses ever satisfactorily explained the stylistic sensibilities of youth either (see, for example, Frith 1983; Bennett 1999).

For such individuals, a need to visually stand out from the crowd has been superseded by a heightened level of reflexive individuality whose articulation is not necessarily contingent on visual style in any obvious sense. Rather, the sociopolitical and aesthetic ideologies drawn from popular musics such as rock and punk appear to have become so ingrained in these individuals' biographical sense of self that they have effectively become an aspect of a more long-term identity or "lifestyle" project (see also Chapter 2). Likewise, among those aging music fans for whom visual style continues to matter as a means of identification with a series of sensibilities and practices drawn from a specific music genre, such individuals tend to consider style first and foremost as an aspect of a lifestyle project that they have worked on over time. Indeed, in this context too, style is also something that has often been reflexively reworked and modified in ways these individuals deem compatible with the aging process and the aging body.

Useful in beginning to map the sensibilities of style exhibited by aging music audiences are ideas emerging from the academic literature on fashion. Influenced by the pioneering ideas of Georg Simmel in the late nineteenth century (see Frisby and Featherstone 1997), such work has concerned itself less with attempting to impose a homological framework over fashion choices, as was the case with much of the early work on youth culture and style (see, for example, Hall and Jefferson 1976; Willis 1978; Hebdige 1979). Instead, fashion research has been far more engaged with understanding the assemblage of fashion items and their display on the body as something bound up with individuals' reflexive understanding of themselves. In this sense, items of fashion become key markers of reflexively constructed lifestyle projects. Thus, according to Gill: "Fashion is an ontological domain; in and through an interaction with fashion *subjectivities* are literally made and worldly relations established between clothes and bodies" (1998: 43).

Similarly, Chaney argues that "fashion literally displays the exercise of taste, an alignment to a sensibility. In the personal choices we make from public vocabularies (that is, fashions), we exercise and display sensibilities that inform and organise choice and taste" (1996: 132–133). Finally, and in keeping with Chaney's observations, Breward suggests that fashion is best understood as "a kind of contemporary Esperanto, immediately accessible across social and geographical boundaries . . . a shorthand for . . . cultural experience or 'lifestyle'" (1995: 229). From the point of view of these and other theorists (see, for example, Barnard 1996; Finkelstein 1996; and Mort 1996), the fashioned body is one that bespeaks an individuality while simultaneously connecting the wearer with like-minded others spread across local, translocal, and global spaces.

Fashion theorists frequently point out that through its connection to reflexive notions of self and identity, fashion may, in addition to its function in accentuating particular physical attributes, also be used to subvert specific aspects of an individual's appearance. Indeed, according to Entwistle, there exists in relation to the fashioned body a palpable "tension between clothes as revealing and clothes as concealing of identity" (2000: 112). Bringing this back to issues of the relationship between visual image and musical taste in a post-youth context, a common assumption has been that fashion is used by the individual subject primarily as a means of masking one's true age and portraying a younger, more youthful image. Significantly, however, more recent studies suggest the possibility of a rather different dynamic at play in the relationship between age, fashion, and identity. Thus, fashion is used not so much as a means of covering up or disguising an aging body. Rather, aging and fashion sense are reflexively interwoven. As individuals age, their fashion sense is subtly modified in ways that closely resonate with and adapt to the changing physical appearance of their aging body.

A useful empirical illustration of this kind of reflexive embodiment of fashion and style in relation to the aging process is offered in a study by Holland (2004) examining the alternative fashion sensibilities of women in their late thirties and early forties. As Holland observes, while her interviewees perceived themselves as at greater risk of stigmatization than their male peers for portraying an "alternative" image as they approached middle age, this did not deter them in their choice of clothing and other fashion attire. That said, subtle changes were evident in the fashion sensibilities of these women as they sought to adapt their chosen visual image to an aging physical appearance. Although many of the women interviewed by Holland experienced a tension within themselves regarding the aging process and the ongoing desire to present themselves as "alternative women," at the same time many professed an ultimate sense of satisfaction in being able to "choose" their identity. Holland's observations are also important in that they offer new empirical insights regarding the changing cultural terrain of fashion and stylistic sensibilities once deemed to be inextricably bound up with youth. For the women featured in Holland's study, the visual images they project may have their roots in earlier allegiances to particular youth cultural styles, but connections between image and age have been reflexively renegotiated, with image taking on new, individually derived meanings as these women have aged. One key indicator of this shift in the meaning of style—and one that is also evident among subsequent accounts included in this chapter—is a move away from style as forming part of a collective identification (as per its common designation in the literature on youth culture) to its role in the construction and articulation of more individualized, ongoing lifestyle projects.

Punk's Not Dead

Such a reflexive awareness of aging as a key element in the (re)construction and articulation of the fashioned self was a recurring point of reference among those individuals interviewed for this book. The accounts provided by aging punks were particularly instructive in this respect. As noted, much of the original literature on punk lays great emphasis on the punk image as a resource for the expression of youthful anger directed at the parent generation and its dominant institutions (Hebdige 1979; Chambers 1985). For example, according to Hebdige (1979), the disintegrating life chances of the British "punk" teenager, a product of the socioeconomic dislocation and the onset of deindustrialization during the mid- to late 1970s, were writ large on the surface of his or her body through the ripping of domestic utility items, such as safety pins and dustbin liners, from their mundane, everyday contexts and reworking them as items of clothing. Punk's visual resonance with the rhetoric of socioeconomic crisis adopted by the British media at this time is similarly commented on by Chambers, who observes:

Punk burst upon an unsuspecting London and quickly acquired the propensity to act as a new folk devil . . . [the] punk's pallid body perforated by safety pins, draped in pvc [sic] and locked in a dog collar; those glassy, amphetamine blocked eyes staring out from beneath shocks of garishly dyed hair. These were the signs that briefly captured the horrified fascination of the outside world. (1985: 175–176)

As such accounts suggest, among the various youth cultural images after the Second World War, punk was by far the most visually dramatic. Significantly, however, among all but a few of the aging punks I interviewed, or was introduced to and talked with in bars and music venues, the extreme dress code associated with late 1970s punk no longer applied in their visual interpretation of the punk image. It was rather the case that selected items, some with more obvious punk associations than others—for example, nose rings, multiple earrings, and metal studs—were worn in conjunction with more casual clothes, typically jeans and a denim jacket. Others exhibited a still more subtle connection with punk, their dress being unrecognizable as in any way associated with punk but for a few sew-on patches or a tattoo with the name and/or logo of a favorite band. Another preferred dress option for older fans of punk was to simply wear black clothing, normally a black T-shirt, jeans, and worn-in Doc Martens or some other brand of fashion boot.[2] Among the older punks themselves, however, such visual displays—no matter how discreet—were sufficient to signify one's affinity with punk and punk music. For example, one evening I accompanied Jim, an English punk in his late forties, to a local punk gig in rural East Kent. During the gig, Jim introduced me to a number of his friends, whom he described as "old punk guys," and added that there were a number of people at the venue that evening whom he didn't know but who were also older punks. Neither Jim nor any of the other people he identified as older punks possessed what could be called a punk image in the more typically understood sense. While I could understand Jim's describing people he knew as "old punk guys,"

---

2. This type of toned-down punk image is also evident among certain older punk musicians, for example, the Washington, D.C., punk band Fugazi.

I was interested to know how Jim could also discern a punk identity among people he didn't know and who, on the surface, appeared to carry no visual markers of punk association. In a follow-up interview several days later, I asked Jim about this. He responded, "You can always tell [an old punk]. Maybe it's just a jacket, or a [sew-on] patch or something . . . just something there that says 'punk,' y'know."

As accounts such as this one suggest, there are continuities between the semiotic qualities of the punk image identified by Hebdige in the 1970s and the ways in which particular items and commodities are identified as "punk" by older punk fans today. Interestingly, however, such semiotic significance has become a restricted code shared only among aging punks. Thus, in the stylistic lexicon of the aging punk, the symbolic value of a residual punk image is intended less as a public visual statement and more as a subtly articulated continuing allegiance to the punk ethos and ideology shared and understood by other aging punks within the local punk scene and/or at various translocal gatherings such as punk festivals.

The hairstyles of older punks were also often a far more subtly articulated derivation of the original and more visually striking punk hairstyles of the 1970s. A typical look among aging male punks was hair that was cut very short, or shaven, with a slightly longer strip of hair in the shape of the classic punk Mohican style. It was evident that, over the years, older punks had refined their image according to their age, retaining an essence of their original punk look but toning this appearance down to the extent that it was acceptable in the context of family, job, and so on but still visually distinctive. As Jed, an English punk in his mid-forties with a seven-year-old daughter, put it: "Being up the school playground I think I'd find it a bit awkward if I had pink hair at the moment." Jed added that he "was going a bit thin on top," a fact that presented him with further problems in attempting to keep up his original punk hairstyle.[3] Several other interviewees commented that they no longer had the time or the inclination to maintain the more extreme punk hairstyles of their youth and that

---

3. A similar sentiment was expressed by a group of aging male fans of the U.S. glam rock band Mötley Crüe at the opening concert of the group's reunion 2005 tour. The fans remarked: "We went from hair bands to lack of hair bands!" (Michel 2005).

their new "toned down" hairstyle was "about right" in that it "sends out the right signal, but [is] low maintenance as well."

Among aging female punks too, examples of a more toned down, "middle-aged" punk image were evident. For example, Jane, an English punk in her late forties, wore her hair in a style reminiscent of Siouxsie Sioux's original late 1970s image but with a very subtle application of gel to produce a slightly spiked look set off by a tint of red and pink. Similarly, Jeanie, an Australian punk in her late forties, had dyed black hair worn in a neater, more stylized version of the shoulder-length bowl-cut hairstyle of U.S. punk group the Ramones, her favorite band.

Although clearly still important as a marker of one's punk associations, this toning down of visual image on the part of aging punks suggests that, as they have aged, their reflexive understanding of themselves as punks has become far more subtly articulated. Their self-association with punk is much less tied to the spectacular style that characterized the original 1970s punk movement and is more individually articulated. This, in turn, may indicate a shift in the way that the notion of commitment to punk alters with age. Thus, rather than commitment being externally communicated though spectacular style, there appears to be a shared understanding among aging punks of having paid one's dues, the proof of commitment to the punk ethos residing not only, or indeed primarily, in the personal appearance of the individual but also in the individual's ongoing, matured punk persona. In other words, from the point of view of older punks, sustained commitment to punk over time has resulted in their literally absorbing the qualities of true "punkness," to the extent that these no longer need to be visually represented through spectacular displays of style on the surface of the body. This corresponds with the findings of Andes in her study of U.S. punks in their late twenties and early thirties. She observes that as punks grow older, the emphasis on rebellion is replaced by an "internal[ization] of punk ideology" (1998: 229).

Aligned with this aspect of long-term commitment to punk is a shifting perception of what it actually means to be a punk. Among the aging punks interviewed for this study, the notion that punk is tied to a form of visual shock tactics appears to have been replaced over the years by a more studied and reflexive understanding of punk as an identity that must be managed and negotiated in the context of other everyday circumstances. Punks who have aged, taken on steady employment, married, and had children now manage their punk identities in combination with a range of other commitments and demands on their time. Thus, rather than setting out to prove one's punkness through the more spectacular forms of visual attire and cultural practice associated with younger punks, aging punks appear to have reached a stage where punk is viewed more as a "lifestyle" (Chaney 1996). For aging punks, the beliefs, practices, and values drawn from punk have become so ingrained that they do not need to be dramatically reconfirmed through the more strikingly visual displays of commitment used by younger punks.

This finding was confirmed by Stu, an English punk in his midforties who had essentially abandoned his original punk image altogether but saw no contradiction between this and the retention of a punk sensibility. In effect, he argued, the dissatisfaction with particular mainstream social values and a desire to articulate his individuality through the visual medium of the punk style had transformed over the years into a "feeling of difference" that emanated from within rather than being expressed through his external, visual image. Thus, Stu observed, reflecting back on the original punk image of his youth:

> At the time, by declaring one way or another, musically, eh visually, that you were something [different], you risk[ed] getting beaten up [laughs], you risked something! Y'know, there was something there. You risked people laughing at you, you risked people sayin' "What you doin' this for, what you doin' that for?" Eh, an' the shock value at the time was the shock of difference, but I suppose the long-term thing was the "sense" of difference, or the individuality that the sense of difference gave you.

This view corresponds directly with those sentiments expressed by respondents in Holland's work (2004) on articulations of "alternative" style among women in their early to mid-forties. Thus, as Holland observes: "A common assertion amongst interviewees was that, although they may have 'toned down' their appearance, they were still the same person ('alternative', 'different') that they had ever been" (2004: 127). Moreover, according to Holland, for some respondents, age had brought with it a new sense of confidence, a new understanding of themselves and their place in the world that did not revolve around the trappings of visual image in the way that it had done during their youth. A corresponding example is seen in Haenfler's account (2006) of older followers of straight edge (or sXe), an emergent youth scene of the early 1980s centering upon hard-core music and a shunning of drugs, alcohol, and sexual promiscuity (see also Wood 1999, 2003). According to Haenfler,

> mature sXers [may] continue to attend shows, enjoy hardcore music, and maintain a sober lifestyle, but most report being less engaged in collective expressions of sXe and more committed to their own lifestyle choices. They settle into the identity, feeling they have less to prove to themselves and others. (2006: 157)

Their shifting notion of what it means to be a punk has also engendered a more critical perception among aging punks of media representations of punk as a spectacular subculture. Thornton (1995) considers at length the role of the media in the creation of "difference" among music- and style-driven youth cultural groups from both inward and outward perspectives. More specifically in relation to punk, Laing (1985) notes how the media played a considerable part in the creation of punk deviance, from the celebrated Bill Grundy interview with the Sex Pistols in 1976, when the British TV host cajoled members of the group to swear on a live, prime-time television program, to the tabloid press's creation of punk as a new moral panic (Savage 1992). While openly conceding that such media portrayals contributed to their own early enthusiasm for punk, aging punks stated that they now saw through such portrayals and critically deconstructed their sensation-making rationale. As with discussions regarding their toned down punk image, when questioned about punk's coverage in the popular press and television news features, aging punks came back to the point that the essence of punk was its longer-term impact on the biography of the individual rather than the sum of its representation in the media. Thus, as Stu contended:

> I think initially there was, y'know at the time, if you wore a safety pin you're a punk, but the image thing is eh ... ultimately, I see that as more contrived. At the time it was great. But, eh, what is the essence of punk? I think it comes back to a psychological thing rather than a superficial clothing thing. . . . The essence of punk, I suppose, is not so much [its] superficial enshrinement ... if you get past the immediate frenzy of how you should be portrayed. It's not about how you look so much as how you feel, how you perceive things, how you act on things, how you do things.

Among the aging punk musicians interviewed, several claimed that their broadening musical vocabulary, together with the diversification of the punk musical style itself, had also had a considerable impact on their attitude toward personal image and how this reflected their sense of punkness. For many, image became less important as their musical taste became broader and more eclectic. Others stated that their developing personal understanding of the relationship between music, image, and outlook had been influenced by joining bands whose style combined punk with elements drawn from other genres of music. This is evident in the following extract from an interview with Pete, an Australian punk singer and guitarist in his late forties:

A.B.: Have you toned your image down over the years?
Pete: I certainly have. I used to have a big screaming mohawk. So I moved on from the image, but certainly the music I hung on to and then searched for more.
A.B.: Why did you leave behind the punk image?
Pete: I got into other bands that had a punk feel, but not a punk look. . . . I got into one band and we were a metal-punk fusion. And really only a punk fusion because of my vocal style.

Again there is a clear sense in Pete's account that his punk identity has, in his view, matured with age to the extent that he no longer regarded it as something that needs to be visually punctuated. Pete also indicates that, although his musical tastes have broadened somewhat over the years, he retains a commitment to music with a "punk feel," this obviously being an important element of his continuing sense of punkness. A further significant aspect of the preceding account is how Pete considers his aging punk identity to be communicated through the vocal style he employs in his music. In his essay "The Grain of the Voice," Barthes describes the "grain" as "the body in the voice as it sings" (1990: 299). Elaborating on this sentiment, Barthes suggests that the voice, when used in song, works as a cultural signifier, bespeaking through its intonation the specific cultural milieu from which it sprang. For Pete, the particular quality of his vocal style not only imprints the punk element on the style of the punk-metal fusion band he refers to in the interview. It is also one of the primary ways in which he continues to self-identify as a punk. For Pete, his voice has taken precedence over punk style as a signifier of his commitment to punk. While image has proved, over the years, to be dispensable, voice has become a permanent embodiment of this aging punk's identity. Although his voice is unobtrusive for much of the time, Pete considers it to be just as immediate a marker of a punk sensibility as a visually stylistic signifier such as hairstyle or dress, when used in the context of live performance.

Once a Hippie . . . ?

A broadly similar, age-adjusted understanding of the resonance between popular music and visual image was evident among respondents who had spent their teenage and early twenty-something years as "hippies" with varying degrees of affiliation to what has loosely been referred to as the counterculture (see Bennett 2001a). Again, age appeared to have brought with it a decreasing concern for the trappings of visual appearance and an increasing emphasis on deeper meanings—political, philosophical, and spiritual—garnered from the hippie experience. Moreover, for some interviewees, the felt need to disengage from aspects of the visual image of hippie culture also appeared to have been motivated by the negative backlash against hippies that set in at the end of the 1960s and found a renewed voice with the successive glam and punk movements of the 1970s (see Laing 1985; Stratton 1986).[4] Indeed, several interviewees claimed to have crossed over into punk, finding there the politicized elements they deemed missing from the counterculture despite the counterculture's rhetoric of social change. In discussing aspects of the hippie style, some interviewees were also quite concerned with what they considered the misrepresentation of the counterculture in the popular imagination. Thornton (1995) has argued that what are often highly differentiated and sectionalized youth cultural affiliations are routinely homogenized and branded by the mass media as coherent groupings. The counterculture has been particularly misrepresented in this respect. According to Clecak (1983), rather than merely expressing a hippie rhetoric of alternativism, as per populist media-driven representations, the counterculture was in reality an umbrella term embracing a variety of groups, including the Civil Rights Movement, the peace and antiwar movements, the burgeoning feminist movement, and environmental groups (see also Bennett 2001a). A number of "aging hippies" were therefore more eager to focus on aspects of their political and/or ideological engagement with the counterculture rather than on their stylistic affiliation (see Chapter 6).

Some interviewees were also noticeably uncomfortable about discussing values and sensibilities they retained from their hippie associations in the context of their current, relatively affluent middle-class lifestyles. Indeed, a number of interviewees did not readily identify themselves as "old" or "aging" hippies at all but rather represented themselves as merely people whose lives had been touched at some level by the hippie values of their youth. Moreover, unlike members of the punk scene, for whom a common excitement in the volume and musical simplicity of punk appeared to have been a primary driver for their teenage involvement in it, those who invested in hippie values suggested in their accounts that even as teenagers they had per-

---

4. Although punk is critically acknowledged as the stylistic and musical reaction to hippie culture, Stratton (1986) has suggested that the image of early 1970s glam rockers constituted in part a satirical send-up of the hippie image, while the musical simplicity of glam rock assumed a proto-punk status in its challenge of countercultural rock's more exhibitionist and self-indulgent aspects.

ceived hippie culture, and their personal associations with it, in a variety of ways. Thus, as John, a middle-class Englishman in his mid-fifties, observed:

> I was fifteen in [19]67, and, for whatever reasons, social, cultural or whatever, the hippie movement really switched me on. I don't think I ever became a real hippie. I wasn't strong enough or confident enough to, ehm, to rebel, I suppose. But the ethos of the hippie appealed to me enormously. The music, the alternative culture, I suppose. Why? I don't know why, because I didn't have a bad home life. It wasn't like I was resisting that in any way. I didn't have a particularly exciting home life. I think I've always been very imaginative and very creative. . . . I like imaginative fiction and surreal paintings, stuff like that. So there's a kind of . . . I'm trying to avoid the word "psychedelic," but that's really what encompasses everything, to me.

Reflecting on how his particular kind of hippie affiliation had impacted on his visual style, John claimed that his dress sense during the later 1960s became essentially what could be referred to as "weekend hippie." At the same time, however, he conceded that his college studies and subsequent early adult life as an aspirant artist and writer, through to the final establishment of a career as an interior designer, had facilitated a creative lifestyle and attendant visual image, characterized by casual dress, that he also associated directly with his early interest in the creative potential of the hippie movement. References to such a casual dress style were common among interviewees in this cohort and serve to confuse the dominant notion of hippie style that has prevailed since the late 1960s. The romanticized, and somewhat stereotypical, benchmark of hippie style was a pastiche of Middle Eastern clothing, DIY tie-dye, and the commercial fashions of hippie "centers" such as Carnaby Street and Haight-Ashbury. The more accurate reality of hippie-affiliated youth was more low-key—a unisex image typified by long hair (for men and women), T-shirts sporting a logo or design, and flared denim jeans. Even the most revered visual documents of the era, such as the movie *Woodstock* (see

Bennett 2004a), attest that the majority of hippie youth adopted such a low-key image instead of the more spectacular style for which the hippie movement has subsequently become known. This fact is supported by the accounts of interviewees, including Mike, an Englishman in his mid-fifties who more readily identified himself as an "old hippie" and had engaged in some of the more widely acknowledged hippie activities, notably traveling the hippie trail to India. As Mike observed: "Well, what was my hippie image? Ehm, well I had long hair and I used to wear flares, but so did everybody else, y'know. It was just the thing to do at the time."

It is perhaps of little surprise then that among my interviewees, accounts of hippie style and how this had impacted on their current visual image tended to be couched less in a context of dressing down, but rather in terms of a more casual dress sense that they had acquired as young adults and endeavored to retain ever since. In some cases, this dress aesthetic was wholly intertwined with a form of identity politics in which visual image and lifestyle were still punctuated by a countercultural aesthetic. Thus, as Jack, an Australian in his early sixties, explained, throughout his life he had tried to avoid working in jobs that would necessitate wearing a suit, as this conflicted with his antiestablishment values. For Jack, such values were crucially articulated through his choice of dress. At the time of the interview, he was wearing jeans, a denim jacket, and a loose-fitting shirt, a style that he claimed to have adopted during his art-school days in the late 1960s and adhered to ever since.

Other interviewees claimed that their sum involvement with youth cultural groups, which in some cases spanned several eras from the 1960s onward, had been accompanied by a sensibility of "anti-style." This is most strikingly exemplified in the following account from Mike (the English interviewee cited previously), who charts his progression from hippie to punk through to his present-day dress aesthetic:

> I stopped wearing flares, but then . . . I was never a particularly typical [hippie], I mean aside from the fact that I had long hair. And yeah, I cut my hair, but I'd done that before punk anyway. . . . Eh, an' I never bought any clothes ever. Whether I was a punk or hippie, y'know, it's still just second-

hand junk shop stuff that I was wearing, an' I still do now, so I haven't changed, y'know.

Although Mike describes his wearing of secondhand clothes as "ordinary" and not essentially connected with a countercultural aesthetic, his observations must be set in the context of larger-scale cultural changes that took place during the 1960s and early 1970s, among them radically new conventions of dress, including the acceptability of secondhand clothes and their significance as a statement of "ordinariness" (McRobbie 1994).

A rather more personalized and emotionally complex account of the relationship between music, style, and aging was offered by Serge, a male French interviewee now in his early fifties and working in a local government position. Having been involved in the countercultural movement during its more radically political phase of the late 1960s and early 1970s, Serge had abandoned the countercultural image altogether while in his thirties. When I interviewed Serge, he presented with short-cropped graying hair, jeans, and a sweater. On the basis of his personal appearance on that occasion, there seemed to be no apparent connection between Serge today and his professed hippie past. Nevertheless, when questioned about his image, Serge claimed that there was a very strong aesthetic continuity between his current image and that of his former, hippie-influenced years. Elaborating on this, Serge noted how, during his teens and twenties, his clothes were often secondhand and non-label makes, this being a palpable expression of his resistance, as a young hippie, to the rampant consumer capitalism he perceived to be around him. Although now enjoying a more affluent, middle-class, middle-aged lifestyle, Serge maintained that the stylistic aesthetic of his youth continued to inform his choice of clothing and the meanings he inscribes to the garments he now wears. As he observed:

> I think the way I dress is more in relation to my political attitude. [And] my political attitude is also related to the music I used to listen to [countercultural rock music]. Eh, I don't wear brand names, I hate brand names. I don't buy running shoes because you can't buy running shoes without a logo. I am

against logos. If I buy a shirt with a name, I just cut the stitch-
ing and remove the logo.[5]

When asked to explain more fully how and why he perceived a
continuity between his current, outwardly conservative style and the
style of his countercultural youth, Serge, like other interviewees before him, contrasted his youth cultural past with a now more internalized sense of difference that no longer relied on the visual shock
tactics of his youth. In Serge's case, this politico-stylistic transition
had been quite extreme. Thus, as he went on to explain, a central feature of his involvement with the counterculture was his interest in
the ideas of left-wing, West German political reactionary Andreas
Baader. Together with accomplice Ulrike Meinhof and others, including Gudrun Ensslin, Horst Mahler, and Irmgard Möller, Baader was a
key member of the Red Army Faction (*Rote Armee Fraktion*), referred
to in its early years as the Baader-Meinhof Group (see Aust 2008). The
Red Army Faction, which became the subject of a major film,[6] was of-
ficially founded in 1970. Referring to itself as a Communist "urban
guerrilla" organization, the Red Army Faction mounted armed attacks and bombings against political targets in West Germany.

Employing a deeply introspective discourse commonly heard
among interviewees when discussing their transition from youth
through early adulthood to middle age, Serge mapped a critical period
in his life when his political views and aspirations began to shift. Although his political principles remained essentially left wing, Serge
had abandoned some of the more radical political ideals of his youth.
Thus, as he explained:

> I used to have long hair. I used to be [both visually and po-
> litically] ugly because I was very influenced by the Andreas
> Baader movement. I was maybe a little bit extreme left at
> that time. I was a little bit apart. But after that, little by little

---

5. Interview was originally conducted in French with assistance from Hervé Glevarec. English translation provided by Hervé Glevarec.

6. Directed by Uli Edel, *The Baader Meinhof Complex* was released in Germany on
September 25, 2008.

I started to wear more ordinary clothes, like eh, [straight-legged] jeans. But before that, I insisted on buying the cheapest jeans in the hypermarket, and it was really ugly.

The concept of ugliness as it is used here is significant in that interviewees rarely described themselves in those terms. For Serge, however, it would appear to be a significant descriptor in his attempts to convey an extreme sense of proximity between dress code and social statement—a conscious attempt to make oneself appear "ugly" in order to challenge the sociopolitical system that existed in Western Europe during the mid-1970s. From this point of view, it becomes easier to see the link between Serge's previous incarnation as a stylized youth reactionary and the deep significance he continues to attach to clothing in middle age. Although far less obviously radical, Serge's approach to selecting clothes—for example, choosing non-brand names—and his minimal yet critical customization of these items—removing logos—retain clearly identifiable traces of a visual aesthetic acquired in youth and subsequently refined and adapted with age. As with some of the aging punks discussed in the earlier part of this chapter, the case of Serge is an example of how a politically oriented project of the self—as promoted through a distinct visual image—has been worked on, refined, and internalized over a period of years to the extent that it is now firmly established as an aspect of an individual lifestyle aesthetic that no longer requires visual punctuation.

Style as "Anti-style"

Thus far, this chapter has focused on what could be described as instances of "classic" youth- and music-based style and the ways in which these have been preserved, modified, or abandoned by aging fans. In conducting the research for this book, however, I also interviewed a number of aging individuals whose stylistic affiliations fell outside the more classic definitions of style. These interviews generated a number of interesting responses to questions of style. Indeed, a number of people refused to equate style as in any way directly bound up with either music or a set of cultural values embedded within a certain style of music. Particularly notable in this respect are comments offered by Mick, an Englishman now in his early fifties, concerning his interest in new wave, a post-punk scene whose most successful exponents have included artists such as Elvis Costello, Joe Jackson, and the Police:[7]

A.B.: How would you describe the new wave style?

Mick: What do you mean by style?

A.B.: Well, the sort of characteristics that made it distinctive in relation to, say, punk or heavy metal.

Mick: Well, this is the thing, you see. I don't reckon there ever was a new wave style. I do remember a bunch of us who were completely cheesed off with all that other stuff, y'know, leather-studded belts, greasy 'air. I mean even punk, that was just so exaggerated, like a bloody pantomime. New wave, well, that was different. It was just ordinary people wearin' ordinary clobber, y'know. Stuff that they liked to wear. I mean, 'ow would you describe Tom Robinson's image with TRB (Tom Robinson Band) as against [Elvis] Costello and Joe Jackson. Nah, it wasn't a style, more like an anti-style really.

A.B.: So would you still consider yourself to be influenced by new wave now, image-wise?

Mick: I think that's the wrong question to be askin' a bloke like me. I reckon "new wave" was just this thing that some music journalist bloke came up with, y'know, course it was, wasn't it? It stands to reason. It was just a convenient way of talking about people like me who 'ad no interest in this idea that music and clothes went together but were more like "I can dress 'ow I want and listen to what I want." It was that simple, and it still is that simple with me.

A.B.: And was, or is, there any political statement behind that?

Mick: Well, politics, clothes, and music, there you go, blah, blah. Since I was sixteen I've always said I'm no different to any other geezer. Nothing's changed.

---

7. In academic writing, new wave has been vastly overshadowed by punk. Indeed, along with New Romantic, new wave constitutes little more than a footnote in the academic exploration of British post-1950 popular cultural history.

For Mick, then, questions of style are not particularly related to musical preference or age. Rather, Mick regards style as an aesthetic statement that is part of an overarching lifestyle politics as relevant in his life now as it was when he was in his late teens. A similar sentiment was offered by Kate, an Englishwoman in her early forties, concerning her ongoing participation in the dance music scene and how this is reflected in her choice of dress, hairstyle, and body modification.

A.B.: Over the years do you think you've adjusted your visual image at all?

Kate: I don't think there's ever been a need to do that really.

A.B.: Can you say a bit more about that?

Kate: Well, I don't think it's ever been about being a "serious" clubber anyway. You know, there are a series of myths about clubbing—it's about being young, rebellious, outrageous, whatever.

A.B.: And you don't think . . .

Kate: Well, no. I mean, yes, there are a lot of young . . . I mean people in their twenties [at dance music events]. But there are people older than me too. But there's no set look as such. I like having my hair a particular way, I like wearing this kind of T-shirt and that kind of bracelet, y'know. There are plenty of people older and younger than me who do the same. Nobody looks out of place. It's more about how you feel. Like having a stud in my nose and a tattoo, it's the same. I'm not trying to be "young" or "fit in" y'know. It's just about who I am. It's about me.

This account echoes responses offered by interviewees in Holland's study (2004) of middle-aged women and alternative style. In both cases, there is no perceived sense that the interviewees are in some way stepping over a line and attempting to occupy a cultural territory in which they have no place. For these women, style is not about youth, or being young, but is rather a critical statement about who they feel they are and how they wish to present themselves. Accounts such as these give credence to Featherstone and Hepworth's notion (1991) of a uni-age style. As Featherstone and Hepworth observe, for individuals born after 1950, new sensibilities relating to the intersection between age, generation, and taste are apparent in which age no longer serves as a barrier to a particular look (see also Chapter 1).

Space, Carnival, Style, and Aging

As the accounts and observations of aging fans thus far reveal, various dimensions of individual agency and subjectivity come into play when deciding how to clothe and present the aging body. Within this, space and place also play a significant role. In particular, gatherings such as festivals, concerts, and dance events offer spaces for the display and articulation of visual style as this relates to the identity of the wearer. Similarly, such spaces offer license to those who wish to preserve a certain aesthetic of visual style and lifestyle politic.

A prominent space for the conspicuous display of stylized bodies is the music festival. The historical significance of festivals as sites of carnival and play is well established (see, for example, Bakhtin 1984). In more recent times, visual documents such as *Woodstock* (see Bennett 2004a) have demonstrated the highly carnivalesque quality of the contemporary popular festival, even as this type of event has become a highly commercialized sphere of leisure and cultural consumption. Indeed, as McKay (1996) argues, music festivals have become nodal points for often highly heterogeneous and multigenerational crowds to gather. Thus, according to McKay (2000), contemporary festivals such as Glastonbury display a rich musical and countercultural legacy, bringing together remnants of the aging hippie, punk, and free party scenes with members of current dance, indie-pop, and world music scenes. As such, festivals also become significant spaces for the reification of particular rituals and practices connected with these various musics and associated scenes—including displays of visual style. A common point made by those interviewed for this book was that festivals were one of the few places where they felt truly comfortable with the way they looked. Others claimed festivals offered an opportunity to "dress up, like in [the] old days." Such sentiments vividly capture a sense in which festivals are considered to retain a countercultural quality that is wholly accepting of carnival behavior, even as the world at large is seen to be increasingly prohibitive in this respect. As Dowd, Liddle, and Nelson observe: "Drawn together from geographically dispersed locations and away from the expectations of everyday life, fans and performers can immerse themselves in a particular culture and experiment with different identities" (2004: 149).

These comments resonate interestingly with the accounts of some of my interviewees. While stopping short of claiming that the festival offered a space for experimentation with "different identities," many suggested that they often felt more comfortable "letting go" in the festival setting, safe in the knowledge that their lifestyle politics, aesthetic preferences, and stylistic sensibilities were in many cases shared or, at the very least, empathized with by others present. Corresponding with the theorization of festivals as a form of translocal scene for the gathering of like-minded others (Dowd, Liddle, and Nelson 2004), many aging fans believed that the festival space was important as a form of affirmation that they were not, in fact, "alone"—that their continuing investment in the visual politics of hippie, punk, or other post-1950s music scenes was part of a "significant minority."

The notion of aging fans coming together to celebrate their continuing aesthetic and stylistic allegiance to particular musical genres and associated scenes in the context of the festival space connotes interesting parallels with Bakhtin's interpretation (1984) of the carnival as part of the "unofficial" culture of any age that blossoms unchecked by the dominant social order. As noted in Chapter 2, the diversification of lifestyles and biographical trajectories that accompany the transition from youth to adulthood can often lead to a sense of isolation for aging music fans, especially among those who continue a keen sense of cultural investment in music as a key aspect of their everyday lives. For such individuals, the festival can provide an important sense of affirmation that their cultural investment is shared by other members of their generation; it can also offer an opportunity to reengage with particular practices—late-night drinking, dancing, recreational drug use, and so on—which, while carried on as individual pursuits, assume more cultural resonance when enacted as a collective practice.

In addition to the opportunities offered by liminal spaces, such as festivals, for expressions of carnival behavior among aging fans, certain geographical spaces are noteworthy. These places have become palpable sites for the establishment and nurturing of alternative life-styles in which visual embodiment through stylistic ensembles of dress, body modification, and so on are common. In such cases, a collective cultural (re)inscription of space and place as a symbolically invested site for particular expressions of stylized identity weaves its own carnival sensibility—one that again operates beyond the control and regulation of the dominant social order.

The Northern Rivers region of northern New South Wales in Australia is an interesting case in point. During the 1970s, the small town of Nimbin in the heart of the region attracted large numbers of hippies because of its isolated, rural location. Within a short period, Nimbin, together with the nearby coastal town of Byron Bay and its environs, became "the alternative lifestyle capital of Australia."[8] Since the 1970s, migration to the region has continued, especially among aging baby boomers seeking alternative, rural lifestyles away from large urban conurbations. In the process, the Northern Rivers has become known for its artists' colonies, organic farming concerns, and cottage industries devoted, for example, to alternative and complementary health products. Byron Bay has one of the few Green mayors in Australia, and the coastal shire has successfully resisted attempts to develop the area as a tourist resort—as has occurred in the adjacent Gold Coast region of southeast Queensland. As this brief overview suggests, sections of the local community in the Northern Rivers have created an environment in which many aspects of the alternative lifestyle envisaged, but never fully realized, by the counterculture have been able to thrive. In many ways, parts of the Northern Rivers exist as what Shields refers to as places on the margin. Moving beyond conventional notions of marginalization, as effected through socio-economic exclusion, Shields seeks to reapply the concept of *margin* to consider how particular places offer avenues for the negotiation of mainstream cultural norms and practices:

> Marginal places, those towns and regions that have been "left behind" in the modern race for progress evoke both nostal-

---

8. See Shea, M. (producer) (2001). *Nimbin, Australia.* Overlander Multimedia. Available at http://www.archive.org/details/Nimbin (accessed January 24, 2009).

gia and fascination. Their marginal status may come from out-of-the-way geographic locations, being the site of illicit or disdained social activities, or being the Other pole to a great cultural centre. . . . They all carry the image, and stigma, of their marginality which becomes indistinguishable from any basic empirical identity they might once have had. From this *primary* ranking of cultural status they might also end up being classified in what geographers have mapped as systems of "centres and peripheries." (1991: 3)

According to Shields, spaces on the margin thus engender alternative norms and practices that embody, to various degrees, conduct and beliefs considered socially and/or culturally deviant in more mainstream spaces. Such a descriptor accurately fits the Northern Rivers. The cultural work that has gone into producing and sustaining a particular kind of cultural milieu in the region is clear when one compares it to the Gold Coast, a space dominated by a highly commodified culture revolving around state-of-the-art shopping centers, entertainment complexes, and Mediterranean-style tourist resorts (Wise 2006). Although in many ways equally commodified, the emphasis in the more bohemian and alternative spaces of the Northern Rivers is largely on countering the perceived excesses of the Gold Coast with lifestyle opportunities that lend themselves to the practice of countercultural values. Within this setting, the original hippie aesthetic, imported into the region by newcomers during the 1970s, continues to thrive and has permeated a great deal of the local culture. It has crossed over into leisure practices such as surfing (the iconic Volkswagen Camper Bus of the original hippie era now being a potent descriptor for the region's "surfie" culture) and also informed the formal and informal economies, from alternative health clinics, cafés, and restaurants to the region's festival culture and street art.

In such a cultural climate, issues of music, aging, and style take on a highly specific and localized resonance. Existing as they do in such a peripheral space, aging members of the countercultural generation have been able to preserve a sense of countercultural distance from the wider society. Although visual style continues to register within this aesthetic, equally important have been the negotiation and sustaining of a cultural space in which the broader lifestyle projects of aging hippies can be enacted on a collective scale. Within such a context, the significance of Shields's concept of the margin becomes clear. Operating within a microculture of countercultural lifestyles, the aging hippies of the Northern Rivers exist in a space that is truly marginalized from the wider society but equally endeavors to marginalize itself through a selective range of cultural practices in which style becomes a dominant demarcator of difference. This is not to say that hippie values have become any less internalized for these individuals than for those discussed previously, for whom visual style has become far less important as a means of articulating a political and/or aesthetic point of view. However, given the process of negotiation and construction of the Northern Rivers as a place on the margin, style becomes a critical resource in articulating a felt sense of distance from mainstream politico-cultural and aesthetic values. Invoking Chaney's related concept (1993) of collective life as a fictionalized process is useful in enabling one to see more closely how the constructedness of space and place within the Northern Rivers constitutes a highly reflexive process. Taking inspiration from the often highly theoretical politics of the counterculture, aging hippies residing in the region have engaged in a process of collectively appropriating and reinscribing their chosen space as a site within which to fully realize and culturally embed their reading of the counterculture's professed political and cultural aims. Within this process, the clothed body becomes a highly important signifier of the aging hippies' reading, understanding, and collective articulation of the Northern Rivers as a space in which they have lived for the last forty-odd years.

As this chapter has illustrated, examining the relationship between music, aging, and stylistic preference reveals a variety of complex and interweaving discourses through which the meaning of style is explained and accounted for by aging individuals. Thus, in some instances, a once visually strident aesthetic of style has been replaced by a more internalized form of identity politics in which stylistic attire is no longer perceived necessary as a means of asserting one's identity. For these individuals, identity has become internalized and forms part of a broader lifestyle aesthetic that does not need to be affirmed through visual style. The toning down of stylized identity thus corresponds to a process of reflection and critical reassessment of the political values and statements once associated with dress. Among other individuals, however, in whom visual style continues to inform their sense of self, this is managed in the context of a discourse that either displaces the fact of being young as a necessary authenticator of visual style or occurs through the development of new "post-youth" means for making sociopolitical statements through dress. Finally, space and place can also be seen to impact on perceived opportunities among some aging individuals to dress in ways that correspond with musical taste and associated political and aesthetic values. Thus, temporal spaces such as festivals, or marginal and peripheral spaces in regional settings, allow for the preservation of "youth" style as part of a broader lifestyle aesthetic among individuals.

4 / Career Opportunities

Work, Leisure, and the
Aging Music Fan

The relationship between popular music, work, and leisure has been only thinly mapped in existing academic work. Part of the problem here arguably relates to an overemphasis on music itself as a source of work and/or revenue. Studies that consider the vocational qualities of popular music tend to focus on musicians (Cohen 1991), DJs (Langlois 1992), and others who make up the infrastructure necessary to support the production, performance, and consumption of music—promoters, club owners, studio producers, record company personal, and so on (Spring 2004; Stahl 2004). Such perceptions of music's value as a vocational pursuit are broadly mirrored in studies of DIY (do-it-yourself) or alternative music industries made possible through digital home-recording technology and Internet communication (see, for example, Smith and Maughan 1998). Clearly, it is essential not to underplay the importance of this body of work. Indeed, prior to the groundbreaking studies of Ruth Finnegan (1989) and Sara Cohen (1991) on local music-making practices, there was little understanding or appreciation of the importance of local music scenes as anything other than training grounds for those aspiring to professional popular music careers (see, for example, Frith 1983).

The point remains, however, that through their continued emphasis on music-making and related spheres of production and dissemination as sources of work in local settings, studies of local music scenes have nurtured a particular perception of music's capacity for the inspiration of career paths. Accompanying this perception is a notion that music lessens in importance, vocationally speaking, as individuals age; thus, we are told, as it becomes increasingly clear to individuals that their youthful dreams of a life in music will not be realized, they gradually leave such dreams behind and opt for more "conventional" careers. Such a view is evident in Andes's study "Growing Up Punk" (1998), in which it is observed that, for punks beyond the age of thirty, the opportunities for remaining involved in the punk scene become more limited, with individuals either leaving the scene altogether or becoming involved in management or production work

This chapter endeavors to broaden the scope of inquiry regarding the intersection between popular music, aging, work, and career path. As the following discussion reveals, the ways in which musical tastes and interests inform work patterns among aging individuals vary considerably. While, for some, the relationship between music and work does indeed cover a familiar and predictable range of activities—for example, musician, songwriter, or record label owner—in other cases music-work relationships take on less obvious, yet equally significant dimensions: music stays at the core of individual lifestyle projects around which work and other elements of everyday life are strategically organized. The range of scenarios portrayed in this chapter suggests something of the depth of meaning that popular music can assume in relation to working life for aging individuals over the course of their lives. Music becomes interwoven into the meaning of work in a variety of ways that are often highly personalized. Indeed, the accounts offered by interviewees in this chapter throw significant new light on the role of music in relation to work, aging, and biographical development.

Doing the "Nine to Five"

As evidenced by the emerging literature on music and everyday life, for the majority of people—that is to say, nonmusicians and others not involved in some direct way with music—the relationship between music and daily activities is often most readily explained in terms of music as background noise—as a soundtrack that accompanies and punctuates the routines of the day (see, for example, Bull 2000, 2005; DeNora 2000). Certainly, when I broached the topic of music and work with aging individuals, this was a common point of entry for them into the conversation. Interestingly, despite music's prominent role in the workplace, little research exists on the topic. This is in contrast to studies of music's role in the broader urban context—including journeys to and from the workplace. In the latter respect, Bull's work (2000, 2005) on the everyday uses of personal stereo and iPod technology has made important contributions to our understanding of how such technologies function as important resources in the negotiation of everyday urban life. Bull's respondents provide compelling and highly diverse accounts of the ways that their daily trips to and from the workplace are supported by personally selected music playlists. The music selections offer an aurally constructed personal space of escape in often crowded public places such as subways and elevators. Bull's work also offers some limited insight into music's place in the work environment through noting respondents' observations that listening to music on the way to work allows them to mentally prepare for confrontations with difficult colleagues in the workplace (see also DeNora 2000).

During my research for this book, I was eager to explore other uses of music and its role and significance in the workplace. The accounts offered by aging music fans provided some intriguing insights into how they had come to regard the importance of music in their working lives. This manifested itself in a variety of ways. Some respondents claimed to have actively chosen career paths that facilitated a constant, everyday immersion in music. Such was the case with Paul, a fifty-year-old man who ran a secondhand record stall at a market in the southeast of England. As Paul observed: "This is the perfect way of making a living for me. It's not many folks who can take their record collection to work [laughs]." Similarly, many respondents claimed to have found long-term career satisfaction in their job primarily "because of" the opportunities it offered for listening to music during the work hours. As Steven, a tradesperson and amateur musician in his late forties and living in South Australia, explained:

> Music means a lot to me; it always has. I really enjoy listening to music. The kind of job I have just allows me to enjoy listening to music all day. As soon as I get to a job, the first thing I do is find a socket and plug in the radio. The music's straight on and it's there with me for the rest of the day. Music is my life. I feel lucky that I've done this job for as long as I have. Y'know, I can just get into and enjoy my music.

Similar observations were often forthcoming from other interviewees. Indeed, tradespeople and others who worked alone were prone to cite the importance of music not merely as a means of passing the time, but also of giving time a different purpose. Free from the need to engage with others in conversation and to coordinate work tasks and schedules, many lone workers claimed that "having music as a work companion" was an important means of reflection and re-evaluation for them. Several interviewees also claimed that it was when engaged in the action of "doing work" that music "came alive" for them, fueling their memories, providing opportunities for retrospection and self-evaluation, and thinking about how their lives had evolved over time and how things might have been different if they had made different decisions in critical moments.

Such was the importance of music in the workplace in this more introspective and emotionally supportive way that it had actually influenced a midlife career change for one interviewee, Pierre, a man in his mid-fifties from a town in northern France. For Pierre, the intrinsic value of work was measured primarily in terms of the opportunities it offered for immersion in a preferred musical soundscape. Thus, as Pierre explained, he had worked as a bartender in the same local bar for over twenty years. The job was easy and stress-free, provided a regular income, and did not require any particular training. More importantly, for Pierre, the bar played the kind of music that he liked—that is, rock and pop-rock music from the late sixties and early seventies. As the clientele of the bar began to change and younger people started drinking there, the proprietor began playing more contemporary styles, such as house and rap, on the bar's sound system. According to Pierre, the change in the soundscape of this and other bars in the neighborhood led him to leave bartending and retrain as an interior decorator. Echoing the sentiments of Steven, mentioned previously, Pierre observed that, although very different from his previous line of work, his new profession was highly satisfying in that it allowed him to create (or in this case resurrect) his preferred personal soundscape—a vital ingredient in making work meaningful through its rendering of work as a time for self-reflection and assessment.

Although seemingly mundane in terms of their operationalization of music in everyday life, such work-based listening practices offer an important insight into the extent to which music can become incorporated into the lifeworld of the aging music fan. In the case of those individuals noted previously, music has not only become a way of making working life meaningful; the domain of working life itself has become recast as a space in which the self is continually reflected upon and enriched through an ongoing dialogue with music. Articulating through their accounts a series of observations corresponding clearly with DeNora's perspective (2000) on music as a means through which to both manage and produce the self, individuals blended discussions of the phenomenological experience of work and the meaning of music within this context in highly tangible and often vivid ways.

Music and DIY "Careerism"

For other interviewees, accounts concerning the significance of music in their working lives centered on how music had been a catalyst for the pursuance of other, more DIY-oriented career paths. Spearheaded by punk, and a reaction in part to the argued romanticism of the hippie culture's concept of alternative living (see Hall 1968; Webster 1976), the DIY ideology assumed its own oppositional mantra. Although initially centered on music-making practices, DIY gradually became a slogan that encapsulated a broader lifestyle outlook and corresponding set of political sensibilities. This broader understanding of the DIY aesthetic was subsequently inherited by the free dance party scene of the late 1980s (McKay 1996) and associated activist groups such as the Anti-Road Protest (Aufheben 1998), Reclaim the Streets (Jordan 1998), and The Land is Ours campaign (Monbiot 1998). McKay defines DIY culture as "a youth-centred and directed cluster of practices . . . a combination of inspiring action, narcissism, youthful arrogance, principle, ahistoricism, idealism, indulgence [and] creativity" (1998: 2). McKay's observations are representative of much of the writing that focuses on aspects of alternative and/or DIY culture, which is regarded as something inherently outside of and antithetical to mainstream culture—and as something inherently "youth centered." However, given the fragmentation of contemporary culture (Chaney 2002) and the increasing prevalence of diverse lifestyles (Chaney 1996) across the social strata (see Chapter 2), such dichotomous readings of society are clearly called into question. Indeed, it is increasingly the case that ready-made distinctions between alternative/DIY and mainstream cultural sensibilities cannot be so neatly drawn. The "youthful antagonisms" that McKay identifies with DIYism may be at the root of individual experiments with DIY lifestyle projects. However, DIYism may also be a sensibility that remains with individuals for the duration of life course, being subject along the way to a continuous process of reflexive adjustment in accordance with the changing outlook and life situation of individuals as they age.

As noted, a critical moment in the evolution of DIY culture was the emergence of punk during the late 1970s. Central to the original punk movement was a strong DIY aesthetic, particularly in relation to the production and performance of punk music. Punk asserted its distance from the "mainstream" commercial music industry through the articulation of a shoestring, no-frills production ethic. In the case of the anarcho-punk scene, this philosophy also extended to the marketing and distribution of music and to touring, with groups such as Crass and Black Flag fixing maximum prices for albums and concert tickets (Gosling 2004). The DIY ethic of punk was also crucial to its performance style. Emphasis was placed squarely on simplicity, in both song structure and musical delivery, punk being in this respect determinedly anti-rock in its stance (Bennett 2001b). Similarly, while hard and progressive rock had by this time become increasingly confined to stadiums and arenas (Lull 1992), punk continued to emphasize the importance of small venues and the interaction with the audience that this afforded (Laing 1985). Despite the accusations of some observers that the commercial success of groups such as the Sex Pistols and the Clash made nonsense of punk's antimaterialist values, DIYism remained strongly associated with punk, particularly from the early 1980s onward, when it once again became a more underground concern. Moreover, the DIY nature of punk was never exclusively connected with music. Stylistically and politically too, punk has always expressed a strong DIY ethic, as seen more recently, for example, through anarcho-punks giving their support to the global anticapitalist movement as well as other single-issue political causes (O'Connor 2002; Gosling 2004).

Accordingly, in speaking about their exposure to punk as teenagers and their continuing association with punk in the present, many aging punks I interviewed suggested that punk's ethos of DIYism had affected them in very deep-seated ways that often surpassed a purely musical dimension. This is, of course, not to downplay the importance of music. Indeed, a number of aging punks indicated that a major aspect of their continued involvement in and enjoyment of punk came through performing in a band. At the same time, however, accounts offered by many aging punks cited music-making as merely one of a range of punk-inspired DIY activities they involved themselves in. The variety of DIY projects engaged in by older punks was strikingly diverse. For example, in Adelaide, South Australia, I met John and Pete, two punks in their late forties who presented their own show on a community radio station. Although primarily a music show, dedicated to playing a mixture of classic punk tracks and new releases, it allowed some limited dialogue between the presenters, primarily as a means of plugging new releases and gigs by local groups. In the following interview extract, John and Pete explain how they became involved in the show and the role they believe it fulfills in the context of the local Adelaide punk scene:

John: Another chap started the show several months before I came on board. And the whole thing of the show back then was to showcase the local [bands]. They got the priority, the local and the interstate bands, the Australian bands.

Pete: And there's always been a lot, hasn't there? There's always been a lot of local stuff.

John: Yeah.

Pete: So there was always a need for [the show].

John: The show started in the middle of 1985, and for some reason, the chap who started it couldn't do it after about two years or so. But I didn't want to see it die, because it was a very good outlet for local bands [and] their music that you wouldn't hear pretty much anywhere else at the time. And . . . I wanted to keep it going. So I've sort of been filling in for the last eighteen years or so [laughs].

Pete: And just as well because it's one of the most popular shows on the station's curriculum now. . . . And we get a fair bit of feedback . . . whether it be from mail or from the phone. People ringing up and saying they're really liking the show and stuff like that.

A.B.: Do you plan to stay involved in the show?

John: Well, this place is pretty much like a second home to me. Yeah, I don't know what I'd do if this place closed tomorrow. It's been a big part of my life.

The preceding account provides a particularly vivid illustration of how the DIY ethos, central to punk's emergence as both a musical and politico-cultural force, has been steadily internalized and personalized by John and Pete throughout their long-term involvement with punk. Although community radio broadcasting may register as a relatively low-key, informally organized activity, for John and Pete it has become a highly important, not to say central, aspect of their lives. They continue to build and develop it, drawing on their well-established knowledge of punk music and their place within the local Adelaide punk scene. In doing so, John and Pete also demonstrate an unbridled commitment to maintaining the show—not because it is a source of income (their involvement in the show is purely voluntary) or necessarily a means to secure kudos for themselves, but rather because they consider the show an essential aspect of the local punk scene. Certainly, a sense of personal attachment is evident in their account of the show. However, rather than suggesting that they themselves are in any way crucial to its survival and appeal, they offer instead a more altruistic account in which they emphasize a mutually shared sense of duty to the show (not wanting "to see it die") and, by definition, the wider, local punk scene and punk music per se.

A strongly ingrained DIY-punk ethos was also articulated by Suzy and Andrew, a second pair of aging punks who also ran their own community radio show. In contrast to John and Pete's program, Suzy and Andrew's show interspersed the playing of punk tracks with a style of talk radio, with each program focusing on a specific topic. Both the topics chosen for discussion and the way in which these were presented embodied a distinctly punk spin, as illustrated in the following interview extract:

A.B.: What sort of topics do you cover on the radio show?
Suzy: We're fairly critical about the Bush administration. . . . We did something about Reclaim the Streets. We do things about . . .
Andrew: Fast food. Y'know, healthy food, sort of organic kinda stuff. Alternative forms of transport . . .
Suzy: So they're alternative takes on issues, I suppose. And we try to present a balance to what's presented in the mainstream as well. To seek the truth about things that people might not necessarily be seeing on the commercial TV news.
Andrew: We try and laugh at stuff as much as possible rather than getting too heavy about it.
Suzy: And [sometimes] people who are listening will phone up and tell us an extra bit of information about something.

Andrew: We often get scientists ring[ing] up and mathematicians, and stuff. When we kind of glibly talk about something we find that there's this fairly intelligent audience out there who can add a lot of stuff. So we'll either get them to phone in on the other line so we can put them to air, or we'll get them to come in the next week or send us articles and stuff.

A.B.: So then the sorts of messages you're broadcasting are getting out there and people are understanding and responding to them?

Suzy: Yeah, and people really like it. One person said to me a couple of weeks ago that ours is the most political program in Adelaide. So, I think that's one of the reasons they're tuning in for it. It's not just the music we're playing. They actually want to hear the things that we're talking about. It's like there isn't much of an outlet for that anywhere else—for people to question the mainstream.

A.B.: So your audience is much wider than purely a punk audience?

Suzy: Oh, yes, very much.

Further conversation with Suzy and Andrew revealed that they had, over the years, developed a considerable portfolio of punk-inspired DIY activities and pursuits. Indeed, such was the extent of these that they had effectively created full-fledged "DIY careers" for themselves. Andrew, who had originally trained to work as a lawyer, became disillusioned with this career and moved into legal-aid work before giving up the profession altogether. Suzy's long-term fascination with radio had led her to train as a radio producer. The two had met through their involvement in community radio and subsequently forged a strong working relationship that extended to a range of other activities. As Suzy explained, "We interview bands and write articles for a street paper—that's a volunteer activity [and] so is doing community radio. And [we] go and see films and write film reviews for a music paper." Picking up on this, Andrew summarized all these activities as being underpinned by what he described as a punk view of the world. He went on to offer the following example.

We write on music and films generally but with a punk perspective [laughs].[1] . . . I mean, you'll go and see a film where
other reviewers have said, "Well, it wasn't that great, but it's
romantic," but that sort of relies on the myth that these people
are going to live happily ever after, and that's how [the film]
ends. An' I just don't buy that stuff anymore.

Conventionally speaking, beyond its outspoken criticisms of
mainstream rock and pop during the 1970s, punk has not been considered to critically engage with mainstream entertainment media.
This undoubtedly relates to the representation of punk, in both academic and popular accounts, as a primarily youth-based concern
with an emphasis on the avoidance of mainstream cultural products.
In this respect, Andrew's reference to viewing mainstream movies
from a "punk perspective" is interesting. It illustrates how a conceptual blueprint for observing and evaluating the world garnered from a
youthful experience of punk has, over the years, been formulated into
a broader set of lifestyle politics, and through these politics, all aspects
of everyday living are experienced and understood.

A further outlet for Suzy and Andrew's continuing commitment to
punk was their involvement in a tribute band dedicated to U.S. punk
band the Ramones. Committed Ramones fans themselves, Suzy, Andrew, and their fellow band member had gone on a number of self-
organized tours, performing extensively across Australia and also in
Europe. Crucial in this respect was the way that Suzy, Andrew, and their
colleague had perfected the art of working casually as a means of sup-
plying a base-level income necessary to sustain themselves, while at the
same time allowing scope for the pursuit of their various DIY projects:

Suzy: None of us works in a full-time permanent job; we've got
casual jobs. So we can decide that we're going to take "that

---

1. This interviewee heard the phrase "punk perspective" quoted in a paper I presented at the Hawke Research Institute while he was a visiting fellow at the University of South Australia. The term was originally coined by another interviewee from
the United Kingdom to describe his critical dissection of news and other current-
affairs television programs (see Chapter 6).

time" off "there." And then we just organized that tour on the Internet ourselves. It was a real DIY thing. In fact, just about everything we do is "do-it-yourself." And that's one of the things that we've got from punk as well, that, if you wanna do something, you just do it yourself.

Andrew: An' do it cheap, do it for nothin'. . . . It's also a priority thing. It's like, when we wanted to go to Brisbane [or] when we decided we wanted to go overseas, we just decided we wanted to do it, so everything else had to fit in with that.

Suzy: Yeah, so we just know that we're not going to spend any money on anything else between now and when we leave because we need to save the money. And we're not going to say yes to other things that will commit our time, which aren't leaning towards us doing this thing with the band. So we prioritize things. And it works.

Another important element in the success of Suzy and Andrew's DIY touring operations with their band was the international networks they had built up through the translocal scene of Ramones fans across the world. In this respect, the Internet had been a crucially important tool, not only in dealing with organizational issues but also in making contact with other aging Ramones fans in a global context.

Thus, as Suzy observed:

We had initially started contacting Ramones fans over the Internet and asking them if they knew of places that we could play in their city, or promoters, or bands who would be doing tours around that time or whatever. And we just kept going, following up contact leads until we found somebody who definitely was going to meet us in Madrid, set up a gig for us, put up the posters, and find us somewhere to stay on that night. And, so we'd get to Madrid and we'd find our guy and we'd do that with him. And, in some places, they'd organized hotels for us to stay in, and in other places we'd just sleep on people's lounge room floors. But what we found was a really great community of people who were very generous and, ehm, sort of nonjudgmental and not really materialistic or anything. But everybody was very friendly and hospitable to us everywhere we went.

Such self-organized tours in turn provided the inspirational basis for another DIY activity. Meeting long-standing Ramones fans from different parts of the world, Suzy and Andrew began to appreciate the variety of ways in which an interest in the Ramones and their music had impacted on the individual biographies of Ramones fans over the years. As they observed, the accounts of aging fans ranged from associating particular tracks with relatively pleasant, mundane experiences, such as meeting their first girlfriend, to more harrowing memories, such as traversing the war zone from Serbia to Croatia during the early 1990s to attend a Ramones concert. Using footage of conversations with Ramones fans recorded with a Hi8 camera while on tour, Suzy and Andrew produced several homemade documentaries to remember such encounters. As Suzy explained:

We took a camera with us . . . to Europe. And we were filming both things for our records like where we were going, what we were seeing, what the venues were like, the people who we were meeting, who were helping us book the shows and so on. But we also saw lots of really interesting music fans there, so we started interviewing them as well and asking them what the Ramones meant in their lives . . . just to sort of document this amazing thing that is still going on even though the band isn't around and three of the original members have died.

While the work and leisure activities of aging punks I encountered were not typically as experimental and DIY as those described previously, ready associations were still made between "lessons learned from punk" and subsequent career choices. For example, Jim, an English punk in his late forties, had elected to work with the homeless, a job that he said, despite its relatively low salary and status and limited promotion prospects, afforded him the satisfaction that he was doing something positive to try to "fix a big problem that the inequalities of the capitalist system ha[ve] produced." The desire to work outside of, or in opposition to, the mainstream world of work and the capitalist logic that it adheres to was shared by Chris, another English punk in his mid-forties, who observed:

> I have never really worked in the straight world; I've always been outside it doing other things. Whether that be . . . making money from putting on a few gigs, or buying and selling stuff on the Internet, all this sort of stuff. . . . I've had two straight jobs in twenty-six years, and all I can remember is complete resentment to[ward] having to be somewhere for eight hours, when I can think of loads of things to do! . . . I often think that work is the last vestige of the unimaginative. . . . To this day, I still want to make money outside of all that. I just think, at the end of the day, that it's the only way that you can maintain control over what you're doing.

A common thread running through this and the following accounts is the way in which individuals from different walks of life, and different continents, have creatively evolved ways of maintaining a DIY-punk aesthetic into middle age. Among the aging punks I met and interviewed, many noted how the anarchic energy that they had identified in punk as teenagers had transformed into a more mature and studied lifestyle project over the years (see also Chapter 6). In the long term, what these people appear to have taken from punk and punk DIYism is a sense of individual autonomy—and this sense was particularly pronounced in expressed attitudes toward work and leisure. Although no longer subscribing to the view that one was free to live completely outside the strictures of capitalism, or in an alternative social setting entirely divorced from mainstream social norms and values, by the same token aging punks were not resigned to accepting the "nine-to-five" routine characteristic of many conventional occupations. Instead, a number of aging punks had literally carved out for themselves DIY careers—occupations that allowed them to generate enough income to get by on but did not tie them down to full-time work and the daily routine that this entails.

"Heritage Rock": DIY Preservationists

Interesting examples of DIY careers were also evident among aging fans of popular music genres not conventionally associated with an ethic of DIYism. A notable case in point is Rob Ayling, an older progressive rock fan who, in 1990, founded his own independent record label, U.K.-based Voiceprint Records. Progressive rock defines a style of music that originated during the 1970s in which elements of rock, blues, and jazz were combined with the traditions of European classical harmony (see Macan 1997). Utilizing studio techniques pioneered by artists such as the Beach Boys and the Beatles, progressive rock groups created highly ambitious concept albums, often containing pieces of music that would last the duration of one side of a vinyl LP (long-playing) record. In a live context, progressive rock was no less grandiose, with groups such as Yes, Genesis, Emerson Lake & Palmer, and Pink Floyd incorporating spectacular light shows and an array of special effects into their live performances. In terms of its commercial success, progressive rock was equally formidable, being something of a corporate giant whose most successful artists had, to paraphrase Frith and Horne, perfected the art of "selling high seriousness" (1987: 73).

The emergence of punk in the mid-1970s and the subsequent rise of MTV with its demand for shorter, more accessible songs heralded the demise of progressive rock. Some progressive rock groups, most notably Genesis, were able to survive in this climate but only through conforming to the new music industry standards that demanded, among other things, shorter, more radio-friendly songs and promotional videos (Martin 1998). Throughout the 1980s, progressive rock was unequivocally branded by music critics as "dinosaur" music. During the 1990s, the genre reclaimed some limited kudos, though this was largely due to the dance music scene's selective sampling from the back catalog of progressive rock and the endorsements of dance-prog fusion acts, such as the Ozric Tentacles (Stump 1997). Even during the period of progressive rock's critical "unpopularity," however, the genre did retain a core of fans who regarded it as inherently more worthy, in terms of its musicality and the artistry of those who performed it, than much of the popular music produced during the 1980s and early 1990s. This sentiment was succinctly summed up by Rob as he explained the rationale for establishing Voiceprint:

> It was the late '80s and early '90s, and the accountants had taken over all the major record companies. So it was all about bean counting essentially. The only way you got people to listen to demos in those days was to tell them that it cost fifty grand, and then it suddenly meant something. Eh, art itself had lost its actual value as art and it was just measured by its cost, y'know. It was the days of lavish videos and, y'know, huge recording bills, and [bands] on yachts zooming across [the sea] to some exotic island. And all the expense meant something as opposed to art itself. . . . So the music which I liked, which was a type of progressive rock, was few and far between and nobody was doing anything.

Writing about the heyday of art rock, the late 1960s precursor to progressive rock, Frith and Horne note how a "commitment to musical truth informed an 'anti-commercialism'" that permeated the aesthetic sensibilities of the art rock scene (1987: 90). To some extent then, Rob's defending of progressive rock as a music worthy of attention because of its artistic intent can be positioned within the context of a rhetoric that has accompanied progressive rock since its inception in the early 1970s. (Fans have regarded this rhetoric as an aesthetic truism in spite of the fact that the dominance of progressive rock during this period was largely assured by the economic viability of its biggest acts rather than purely by their artistic quality.) At the same time, however, Rob's particular knowledge of progressive rock, one built up through a long period of fan involvement with the genre, belies a far more finely nuanced understanding and perception of the music and what it was deemed to stand for. This includes a knowledge and appreciation of the contribution of artists whose names and recordings barely register in canonical definitions of progressive rock and whose lower-profile careers pitched them well below the radar of commercial success and critical acclaim enjoyed by the more famous exponents of the progressive rock genre. As Rob points out, many such artists have lived much of their lives in relative obscurity, an issue exacerbated during the digital revolution of the mid-1980s. At that time, CD replaced vinyl as the preferred format for commercial music releases, and record companies began deleting albums from their existing vinyl catalogs, dropping artists who were no longer considered to be commercially viable. A growing awareness of how this development had affected the musical careers of such artists was instrumental in Rob's decision to establish Voiceprint:

> I started working with an outfit called The Gong Appreciation Society. And it was just a part-time labor of love. The [previous organizer] gave it to me and said, "Look, I don't want it to die, [so] maybe you could keep it going a little bit." Along with that came the responsibility of looking after names and addresses [of people like] Daevid Allen, a former member of Gong [whose] contact details I'd never had before. So, my joyful naïveté meant that I phoned him up in Australia and said, "I can't buy your records, why have you stopped making records, why have you stopped recording?" y'know. And he ha[dn't] stopped recording, but the major record companies ha[d] stopped releasing [his work]. And the indies weren't that interested in that sort of thing anyway 'cause, y'know, it's like a guy on the other side of the planet who was in a band in 1969, who had a vague chart success and had a couple of psychedelic albums on the Virgin label. Nobody was really that interested. CD was still a little bit in its infancy, all the obvious stuff had been reissued like *Dark Side of the Moon*. Y'know, things like that or the Beatles, or Genesis. But nobody had really got into the swing of putting out unreleased things, all that sort of stuff.

There was a further dimension to Rob's investment of his time, energy, and personal passion for progressive rock in this way. This related to his understanding and interpretation of the longer-term implications of the music industry's ongoing concern with the rationalization and streamlining of its production and marketing strategies. For Rob, this established trend—which he only half-jokingly referred to as the "accountant rock" mentality—threatens to eradicate from public view, and consequently knowledge, crucial aspects of popular music history. It also jeopardizes the work of artists who have contributed to the development of particular genres, including progressive rock. Thus, as Rob explained:

> [With] accountant rock, the heritage sort of thing dropped under the radar. The way major record companies are structured is that each individual department has to make a profit, and each different territory has to make a profit. So, you release a Daevid Allen reissue which sells five hundred copies [and] they can't even pay the bills of their internal costs. . . . So subsequently, small things like Daevid Allen or Gong, or whatever, just got completely overlooked. That's the accountancy mentality.

The concept of "heritage" in this context is significant in that it connotes an equation of rock, an ostensibly commercial product, with notions of art and culture, which are generally regarded as quite separate from the forms of commercial culture produced by the mainstream cultural industries (Shuker 2001). As observed in Chapter 1, with the aging profile of its audience, the music industry's retro arm is increasingly a key aspect of its business concerns. Major rock acts of the late 1960s and early 1970s are enjoying a revival of their commercial success via the elaborate repackaging and re-release of "classic material." Such ventures are supported by a broader retro industry as seen, for example, with the highly successful television series *Classic Albums* and the spin-off concept *Classic Albums Live* (see Bennett 2008a, 2009; Bennett and Baker 2010). Significantly, however, Rob's use of the term "heritage" in the context of rock marks an air of resistance to the overtly economic rationale underpinning the music industry's retro-marketing campaign. In positioning the sanctity of the "heritage act," that is to say, artists and groups who have "dropped under the radar," as a core ideology underpinning the establishment of Voiceprint, Rob is simultaneously making a statement concerning the perceived importance of art over economics in the understanding and representation of rock history.

A key rationale for launching Voiceprint was then, according to Rob, to provide exposure for those artists and recordings that no longer attract the interest of mainstream record companies. However, this reasoning is also critically underpinned by Rob's and his label colleagues' sense of affinity with the translocal scene of aging progressive rock enthusiasts around the world. As Rob explained:

> We had a company round at the office who wanted to promote their marketing services. And we said, "We're too specialist for you to actually suggest what we do. The information we require we get directly from the people we sell to." And it's a very personal relationship we have with our public, y'know. . . . The Internet's made that a lot easier. . . . So I don't actually have to be at a showcase or a gig or anything to do that. We can just be e-mailed. People can say, "Why don't you do this?" or "Why don't you do that?" I think it's a case of making yourself accessible, y'know. . . . I think it's [a case of] small is beautiful, with what we do. It's small enough to react to people's wishes and requirements and actually get a positive reaction.

In the preceding account, Rob expresses a view that would, on the surface, appear to have more in common with the discourse of punk or indie than the ethos of a label specializing in the marketing of progressive rock. Moreover, this type of discourse is far more readily aligned, in the popular imagination, with young music fans rather than those in middle age and older. Indeed, in many ways, the preceding vignette begins to debunk another popular media stereotype of the aging rock fan, that is, as someone whose musical tastes are dictated by the "*Rolling Stone* history of rock and roll" and whose record-shopping habits are thus confined to mainstream outlets such as Virgin Megastore and MTV (Hayes 2006: 64). Such a stereotype is less than sympathetic to those older rock fans whose more specialized musical tastes prompt them, as demonstrated here, to source their music via other means. Nor does it aid in understanding the diversity of tastes catered to by such alternative outlets and the types of scene dynamic underpinning those who subscribe to and communicate via such alternative, online patterns of consumption.

As noted, Rob's commitment to Voiceprint and the ethos supporting the label was very much informed by a reflexive positioning of himself as part of a translocally situated scene of aging progressive rock enthusiasts. Correspondingly, Rob displays a highly developed, affective understanding of the cultural and political cohesiveness of this scene, the common preference for progressive rock being underscored by a range of other commonly cherished lifestyle preferences and political dispositions. Reinforcing the observations made in Chapter 2 regarding the affective qualities of music scenes, Rob's sense of belonging in this case is not based on face-to-face contact, or indeed personal knowledge of other aging progressive rock fans. Rather, it derives from an intuitive sense of shared generational memories, experience, and resultant lifestyle and everyday outlook. Such sentiments were clearly evident when I asked Rob about the target market for Voiceprint. In response, Rob offered the following observation:

> This is the wonderful twist, you see, the target market is me. Eh, I kind of look at the things which I do as a way of accessing people like myself. Y'know, I listen to Radio 4 a little bit; I listen to a bit of Radio 2. . . . I read the *Independent*; I spend a lot of time on the Internet. I don't read *Q* magazine because it's just a yuppie coffee-table magazine. And I do read *Mojo*, y'know. I read retrospective [publications]. So I kind of look at myself as my target group.

As this case illustrates, for DIY music preservationists, a deep sense of commitment to music is often presaged by an affinity with music, and a broader cultural milieu, which goes well beyond the listening experience. For these individuals, music has become a barometer for their stock estimations of value and authenticity in everyday life. For Rob, living through the 1980s and early 1990s is colored by his disillusionment at the dawning of the yuppie era—of which one personally painful facet was an increasingly calculated commodification of music. In this respect, his DIY efforts to preserve progressive rock (which he considers a last bastion of art in the face of "accountant rock's" colonization of the popular music industry) become part of a lifestyle project—a way of paying back a debt—as progressive rock had enriched his life and the lives of others.

It was not, of course, the case that DIY career paths such as those described previously were open, or indeed attractive, to everyone who participated in the research for this book. However, even among some of those research participants who existed in what the interviewee Chris referred to as the "straight world," music played a big part in the way they managed and negotiated their working lives—and in some cases provided for them a meaningful link between work and leisure.

Sustainable Fun

When discussing the relationship between work and leisure, and the importance of music within this, a number of interviewees spoke of music's significance in relation to what they referred to as "sustainable fun." Interestingly, this phrase was often heard in interviews with aging followers of electronic dance music. Although it is increasingly evident that the age range of the dance music audience now extends well beyond "youth" in the conventional meaning of the term, in academic studies of dance music, little attention has been paid to this issue.[2] Rather, the subversiveness of dance music is linked almost exclusively to its perceived "subcultural" cachet for a youth audience (Redhead 1990, 1993). Empirically speaking too, dance music followers are primarily represented as a youth-based audience whose "older" members are barely into their thirties (see, for example, Malbon 1999).

Likewise, if much scholarship on dance music rejects the tenets of the Birmingham Centre for Contemporary Cultural Studies (CCCS) subcultural theory in favor of more contemporary, postmodern-influenced writers such as Maffesoli (1996; see also Chapter 2), many researchers of dance music continue to draw on subcultural discourses of resistance, linking this resistance to practices of hedonism and

---

2. For an exception to this trend, see Gregory (2009).

escape (see, for example, Melechi 1993). This aspect of dance music culture is said to be accentuated by the socioeconomic context of its origins—that is, postindustrialization and the concomitant emergence of a new leisure society. In such a context, youths' exposure to casual labor, unemployment, or increasing involvement in higher education is argued to offer the advantage of a relatively unstructured lifestyle, and thus more scope for regular participation in clubbing (Thornton 1995). Arguably, however, it is erroneous to claim that all individuals who frequent dance clubs or participate in the wider culture of dance music fit into this category. Contemporary dance music has, in truth, attracted individuals from a many different walks of life; additionally, the contemporary dance club scene is distinctly multigenerational (Bennett 2000). Moreover, many older members of the dance club scene pursue high-powered professions—as lawyers, doctors, and so on. For such individuals, the relationship between work and clubbing embodies an obvious, and in many ways precarious, series of contradictions. Indeed, for those with professional careers and responsibilities, the practice of clubbing demands an altogether different form of commitment—together with a high level of self-discipline—in order that two very different lives can be managed and maintained.

Speaking about his involvement in the London dance club scene, along with two friends of similar age to himself, Simon, an international property consultant in his late forties, offered the following account:

> I was working in a nine-to-five job. So were my two friends. Y'know, we were pulling down good salaries and doing grown-up things. But on Friday we were going out, and we'd go out from Friday night usually until Saturday evening, sometimes Sunday lunchtime. Just going all the way through. And then driving back, recovering on Sunday evening, and then going back into work again on the Monday. And we would do that three, sometimes, four weekends a month.

Thornton has suggested that older adults are often drawn to dance music and other "youth cultural" scenes as a means through which to resist "social aging [and] resigning oneself to one's position in a highly stratified society" (1995: 102; see also Du Bois-Reymond 1998). On one level, Simon's account lends credence to Thornton's observation, his reference to "doing grown-up things" suggesting that he and his friends simultaneously seek a diversion from such commitments through their involvement in the dance club scene. At the same time, however, further comments offered by Simon demonstrated a more complex interplay between his work and leisure life in which his relatively high-profile socioeconomic position was actually regarded as integral to the pursuance of a satisfying lifestyle. For Simon, his age and responsibility necessitated a rigidly adhered to series of checks and balances, particularly in relation to basic issues of health and well-being. While clubbing is a key leisure activity for Simon, it is also an activity that has to be carefully managed; clubbing is thus regarded as merely one component of a meticulously coordinated lifestyle project in which each element is as important as the next in the maintenance of sustainable fun. This was clearly articulated in Simon's expressed attitudes toward drugs and how these had changed over the years:

> You have to go one of two ways. You either lose it or you go into some kind of mark of craziness because, y'know, it does fiddle with your system. You have to step back and go, phew. There are two things I would never do, that's heroin and crack. But I've done everything else, sensibly. Because it enhances it. You know, it makes the journey more pleasant. [But it] isn't a destination in itself. . . . and those people who confuse the journey with the destination are the people who get lost along the way. And end up in rehab. And I don't intend to do that, because I've got a wonderful life. I can stick two fingers up at the establishment in the nicest possible way. I ask for nothing more.

According to Simon, another major factor in his successful management of clubbing activities and professional workplace responsibilities was the sense of continuity he experienced between his work and leisure spheres. A key element in this, suggested Simon, was the fact that his employer was also an experienced clubber, and thus both understood and shared Simon's commitment to the club scene. According to Simon, while dance music and clubbing were rarely topics of conversation between them, the fact that both he and his employer pursued and managed their lifestyles in similar ways had created a strong bond of trust and collegiality between them. As Simon observed:

> My boss can say he's taking time off and won't be back until Tuesday next week. I know exactly what he wants and how he's going to go about getting it. But he also knows that . . . because I party in the same way that he does that he can trust me implicitly in terms of presenting a professional face for the company on Monday morning when I'm running it while he's not there. And, for me that's fantastic . . . to actually have that as a thread running, not just through your social and your personal life but through your working life as well.

The importance of sustainable fun was also pointedly emphasized by other aging dance music followers involved in the organization of free parties. As with clubbing, the typical representation of the free party scene—which involves all-night free parties that are usually held in marginal spaces such as disused warehouses or outdoors in the woods (Chatterton and Hollands 2003)—suggests that this is sustained largely by those whose lives are not bound by the strictures of full-time employment, regular working hours, and their associated demands and responsibilities. Again, such representations are to some extent guided by the perception of the free party scene as youth dominated (see, for example, McKay 1996). The following account offered by Neil, a party organizer and DJ in his mid-forties, portrays an altogether different scenario. Like Simon, Neil suggested that, as an older dance music enthusiast with work and domestic responsibilities to consider, the key to his success in and enjoyment of the free party scene was a continual balancing of priorities. Moreover, as Neil went on to explain, although arranging parties involves a great deal of commitment, parties are only one aspect of his life and have to be managed in relation to other, more important commitments, including the coordination of several part-time jobs.

A.B.: How do you fit the rest of your life in around [organizing parties], because it sounds quite time-intensive?

Neil: I think because it's teamwork. . . . If I was doin' it all on my own, then I wouldn't be able to do it. I have two jobs that I do, an' I have them as my priority really.

A.B.: Your jobs are your priority?

Neil: Yes, my jobs are my priority [laughs]. The parties don't pay the bills, really.

Neil then offered some candid observations on the difficult process of managing an aging body in the context of a scene that places a high level of emphasis on physical exertion over long periods of time and during hours that would normally be spent sleeping. In talking about the extreme physical demands that his lifestyle placed on him, and how these increased as he grew older, Neil described the strategy he had adopted for coping with them:

> You're stayin' awake all Saturday night and then gettin' to bed, say midday Sunday. I might have four hours sleep, wake up, 'ave something to eat, and then go back to bed again. Try to get ready for Monday mornin'. An' you're just knackered really, so Monday can be a bit rough. So you 'ave an early night Monday to make up them two or three hours that you didn't get on Saturday night.

Such accounts are noticeably out of step with descriptions of the dance scene that portray it as a space exclusively reserved for the exertion of youthful energy buoyed by a twenty-four-hour party lifestyle. Rather, they bring a new dimension to our understanding of the contemporary dance scene and those involved in it. Assuming the "rightness" and "naturalness" of taking their lifestyle preferences forward with them into middle age, all of the aging dance music enthusiasts discussed previously show themselves to be confronted with a common challenge: how to adapt to the demands of the dance and party scene with an aging body and the added responsibilities that age has brought with it. This challenge has in turn necessitated a new lifestyle project—that of achieving and maintaining sustainable fun.

Music, Midlife Career Moves, and the "Reincarnation" of the Self

In the last twenty years, much has been written about the increasing level of risk and uncertainty in late modern, postindustrial societies. Beck (1992), who is generally credited with coining the term "risk society," claimed this society to be the by-product of a new age in which the life course of individuals was subject to an uncertain future. This uncertainty was due, among other things, to increasing instability in family structure, elongated transitions from youth to adulthood, unpredictable economic shifts, and the rising probability of environmental catastrophes. One potential upshot of risk societies, argued Beck, was a new age of individualism in which social actors, less constrained by social structures, are increasingly inclined to pursue individualist agendas in the pursuit of happiness and well-being. The development of Beck's ideas in contemporary social theory has seen them deployed in largely negative terms, for example, in the work of Furedi (1997). According to Furedi, risk and uncertainty are deemed to go hand in hand with a wholesale retreat from public life as individuals become locked into a "culture of fear."

Accounts offered by interviewees in the research for this book occasionally pointed to different ways of understanding the significance of risk and uncertainty in everyday life and the attendant culture of individualism this is seen to propagate. More pointedly, such accounts suggested that the new sensibilities of aging evident among many interviewees—and the ways in which these impacted on previously dominant benchmarks of achievement in terms of socioeconomic status, financial security, and career progression—may also be unraveling. As a result, aging individuals are prepared to take more risks in the pursuit of an aesthetically fulfilling lifestyle. Such was the case with Alex, an Australian woman in her late forties who was in the process of leaving the medical profession to focus full-time on songwriting and performance. The first, and critical, decision in this respect had been to move from full-time to part-time work as a means of giving herself more scope to develop her skills as a songwriter and live performer. As Alex explained, although this change considerably reduced her material standard of living, she viewed any disadvantage associated with it to be offset by the new levels of creative freedom she was able to enjoy. Thus, as she observed: "I feel like I'm actually being reincarnated in a second career [as a musician and songwriter]."

When asked about the extent to which age had been an issue in her decision to make such a significant career change, Alex offered an interesting response. Although acknowledging the somewhat unconventional nature of her decision, Alex believed that the economic risks involved were offset by a freedom to creatively engage with issues of age, life course, and lifestyle preference, and act in accordance with an intuitive sense of what direction she felt her life should go in. Thus, she observed: "I'm really aware that it's a very unusual thing to try and start a music career in your forties. . . . Although I kind of grieve the loss of having done this earlier, when I was doing other things, there is no point at which I'll be as young as I am now."

Expanding on this last observation, Alex explained how it was only through age and accumulated life experience that she was able to critically reassess her life course trajectory and to make the changes necessary to construct a new lifestyle project in which work, leisure, satisfaction, and well-being became more closely aligned. Indeed, when she discussed her new lifestyle in such terms, it became clear that, as with many others interviewed for this book, she saw age as a distinct advantage. This sentiment was echoed by Helen when she discussed her songwriting aspirations and the value that she felt life experience could bring to this activity:

> I think I'm very lucky that songwriting's my thing and that basically when someone in America hears the song they're not seeing what you look like, they're not seeing your image, they're actually after the song. So that part of music-life experience actually seems to be a bit of an asset. And an ability to write in a way that's a bit less clichéd, and a bit less juvenile, if you like [laughs].

Although in many ways she was making individual decisions about how to reconfigure the relationship between work and lifestyle, Alex's everyday sociocultural milieu was also of clear importance for her in evaluating her new career project, and indeed her self-perception as a "reincarnated" individual. In my own work (see Bennett 1997, 2000) and that of Cohen (1991), the significance of music-making as a means of communicating a shared sense of local identity and experience between musicians and audience has been critically underscored. Alex explains how her relationship with her peers, punctuated by her local live performances in clubs and bars, adds a new element to this understanding of local music-making's place as a medium for sociality. It throws light on the age-related dimensions of such cultural exchange. As Alex observed:

> I'll get my peers, and I'll get my peers' parents, sometimes. . . . I think the primary reaction of people is celebratory 'cause people think, "Isn't she happy? She slaved away for all those years." Finally she gets to do what she really wants to and just gets on and enjoys it. And people have been just immensely supportive.

In many ways, the preceding account demonstrates the very "social" aspect of Alex's newfound career path and the enhanced connections it creates between her and her peers. For Alex, the articulation of her new career and attendant lifestyle critically involves the participation of her peers. Such participation in turn rests upon an understanding among Alex's peers that her music and performance are a very localized and intimate form of sociality underpinned by Alex's song craft; this is interpreted as a celebratory statement of an aging group of friends moving along the life course together, sharing in the experience of getting older. As Alex commented with reference to members of her peer-group audience:

> I think they quite like that I quote them in the songs [laughs]. I think they quite like that I've become quite eccentric and I carry a notebook and they say profound things and I write them down and quote them in songs. And I think there's just some sort of amusement at this strange person that I seem to be evolving into as I get older.

The preceding observation again exemplifies a new sensibility of aging and its articulation through music. In many ways, the case of Alex, her career change, and the response of her peers gives further credence to the importance of music as a cultural platform for the rearticulation of the aging process, because it inscribes it with a new set of expectations centering on a collective desire among aging individuals for new lifestyle experiences and associated opportunities for fulfillment.

This chapter has focused on the relationship between music, work, and leisure as this is envisaged and enacted by aging popular music fans. Going beyond conventional notions of popular music's significance in relation to work and career path, the chapter has endeavored to illustrate how, in addition to activities such as music-making, connections between music and work may take on a range of less obvious, yet equally important, dimensions for social actors as they seek to embody music within their everyday activities and cultural practices. In this context, it has been observed that music may be harnessed as a means of negotiating the workplace and/or making work more meaningful. Similarly, the workplace itself may, through the medium of music, be made into a space for critical reflection and self-assessment. Music may also provide the political and/or aesthetic impetus for a DIY career path or one geared toward the presentation of a particular music scene or aspect of popular music heritage. Similarly, an interest in music-making and performance may inspire wholesale career moves for older individuals seeking a more creative and personally fulfilling lifestyle, despite being established in professional careers that provide material rewards and comfort.

5 / "This Is 'Dad House'"

Continuity and Conflict among
Multigenerational Music Audiences

Throughout this book, it has been noted occasionally how many of those popular music scenes that continue to be categorized under the banner of youth culture are now, in fact, essentially multigenerational. The existence of common tastes in popular music, style, and attendant cultural resources across the generations has led to claims that the concept of youth, as a stylistically demarcated cultural category, no longer exists; that youth now describes a way of feeling as much as a way of being (Osgerby 2008). Such observations, however, tend to oversimplify a process of cultural change that is far more complex. Thus, while continuities may now exist across the generations in terms of musical taste and associated stylistic sensibilities, these often engender their own generationally marked tensions. Most obviously, the fact of generation can, in itself, produce a particular perception of the meaning and significance of a specific music genre. For example, and as will presently be considered in more detail, aging members of the punk audience often argue that their experience of the original punk scene of the late 1970s makes for a unique understanding of punk. It is one that differs from that acquired by younger fans who have been introduced to punk music and its associated style during the 1990s or early 2000s. Arguably then, the meanings attached to music are, to some extent, grounded in issues of time and place. This, in turn, may produce conflicts across different generations of fans, especially in relation to discourses of "authenticity." While such discourses—and the conflicts they engender—are a facet of every popular music scene, they may be exacerbated in those scenes with a multigenerational fan base.

At the same time, however, it is important to note that not all multigenerational associations involving the consumption and cultural understanding of popular music embody conflict. On the contrary, popular music can also be a rich source of intergenerational bonding, particularly between parents and children. In a review of a performance by British progressive rock group Pink Floyd at London's Earls Court in 1994, music journalist Adam Sweeting observed: "IT ISN'T JUST the 30-to-50-somethings who are flocking Floydwards. There's a new generation of listeners in their teens and twenties, who have been brought up to revere the Pink Floyd imprimatur by parents or older siblings" (1994: 8). The generational trading of musical tastes and influences alluded to by Sweeting is further investigated in my own work on the Benwell Floyd, a young Pink Floyd tribute band from Newcastle, United Kingdom, whose primary source of musical inspiration had been supplied through family networks and their facilitation of what I refer to as an "informal music education" (Bennett 2000: 181). Elsewhere I have noted how musical tastes inherited in this way have become the bedrock for other leisure pursuits, such as family outings to local pubs and bars where live music is performed (Bennett 1997). Similarly, American author Peter Smith (2004) describes how sharing an interest in the music of the Beatles with his son became a vehicle for other pursuits, including, for example, trips to England to visit Beatles-related tourist attractions in Liverpool and London.

The Golden Age of Youth

A critical turning point in the relationship between popular music, politics, and lifestyle occurred in the mid-1960s with the emergence of psychedelia and the hippie counterculture. Also, often exaggerated (see Chapter 6), the impact of popular music on baby-boomer youth during this period has been the subject of a large volume of work, both popular and academic (see, for example, Wolfe 1968; Reich 1971; Thompson 1993). The sheer amount written about the mid- to late 1960s and the music and youth culture of this era has arguably done much to shape popular perceptions and also significantly influenced the collective cultural memory of the baby-boomer generation per se. Writing during the mid-1990s, American cultural theorist George Lipsitz offered a searing criticism of the aging baby-boomer generation because of what he regarded its obsessive fascination with the time of its own youth—the 1960s. Thus, observed Lipsitz:

> Contemporary discussions of youth culture seem particularly plagued by memories of the 1960s—as if nothing significant has happened over the past twenty years. To be sure, the 1960s deserve recognition as a decade when young people active in the civil rights movement, in student protest groups, in antiwar activity, and in the emergence of the women's liberation took history into their own hands and provoked substantive changes in society at large. But the enduring hold of the 1960s on the imagination of the present has been pernicious. (1994: 17)

Lipsitz's comments are given credence by a flurry of articles that appeared around the same period in which baby-boomer journalists were seen to represent their youth as a golden age (Bennett 2001a, 2007). Inherent in their glorification of this period was a critical lament about contemporary youth, who, it was claimed, had produced no credible icons, no credible music, and, crucially, no distinctive youth culture of their own (see, for example, Forrest 1994). More than a decade later, such perceptions are still clearly in evidence among some members of the baby-boomer generation. A recurring theme in interviews conducted with aging baby boomers was the comparisons they made between their own experiences of youth and what they judged to be the current youth experience. Invariably, this difference was articulated in terms of attitudes toward and cultural understandings of popular music, as these were perceived to have shifted between the generations. John, an Englishman in his mid-fifties, offered the following observation:

> I think music is still important to [contemporary youth], but I think in a different way than it was to me and my generation. To them it's kind of like, y'know, the right kind of hamburger, or the right kind of mobile phone to have, or the right kind of T-shirt to wear or whatever. It's the band or the artist that you like. I think it was much more the music in our day.

Similarly, there was a widespread belief among members of the baby-boomer and, indeed, post-boomer generations that what they had experienced as teenagers and early twenty-somethings was a watershed period in the history of post-1945 youth—one marked by a discernible generation gap in which age-related attitudes toward popular music and its associated stylistic innovations played a fundamental role. Some individuals further argued that such a generation gap was entirely absent in contemporary society because of the faster circulation of popular music genres and associated commodities and the increasing proximity of taste patterns exhibited by youth and the parent culture. This sentiment is clear in the following account from Simon, an English dance music fan in his mid-forties:

> When I grew up, I at least could rebel against my parents. My parents' values, my parents' music stank. And I could say, "Hey, listen to this." Y'know, it was 1977, I've got punk, I've got the Clash, I've got the whole thing. I'm seventeen years old, fantastic! Now, kids can't do that because it's moving down. The parents are appropriating their [children's] music, which pushes [the children] often into the more extreme ends of stuff just to ensure that the parents don't dig it. But that said . . . they're doing it because they can rather than because they want to, I think!

This account is significant for a number of reasons. First, the interviewee contributes what he regards as a shifting terrain of musical appreciation on the part of youth to a colonization of its once clearly delineated musico-cultural space by the parent generation. This, in turn, leads the interviewee to surmise that youth's only means of resistance is a collective resort to more "extreme" forms of music. While such exclamations of youth musics as "noise" are by no means new, what is significant in this observation is the interviewee's implication that "noise" has become an end in itself in contemporary youth music. From this point of view, it is not only the music that has been appropriated by older generations but also the ability to read music in socially and culturally "meaningful" ways. This kind of sentiment is also evident in the following account provided by Jo, a female Australian punk in her late thirties. Lamenting what she perceives to be a misconception among younger generations of fans about punk music and its underlying ethos, Jo said:

> Today's youth find the appeal in punk rock of mindless violence. What they don't realize is that while the music itself can be perceived as violent, the culture itself is not. . . . The mosh pit[1] at gigs was never anything more than a gestalt animal of a group of music fans united by the sounds and energy of the music. Today's fans are into the music and what they perceive the scene to be because they see in it an umbrella reason for violence and bad behavior, not anything more. They don't seem to understand that the punk scene was—will always be—a place where those of us who are essentially out of place or loners come together with like-minded people to enjoy this music and to form a bond with others.

On one level, observations such as these could be construed as a failure on the part of older generations to appreciate the way in which the sensibilities of youth are always in part a product of socioeconomic

---

1. The term "mosh pit" denotes the floor space immediately in front of the stage, or spot where a band is performing, where members of the audience engage in a style of dance referred to as moshing. It involves keeping the body bent over and compact and swinging either one or both arms across the body. Moshers regularly collide with each other and are flung to the floor, to be picked up by other moshers in the pit. For a fuller account of moshing, see Tsitsos (1999).

experience (Grossberg 1994). Thus, what Jo construes as "mindless violence" on the part of younger punks may, in the cultural lexicon of contemporary punk behavior, conform with a codified system of behavior. That system of behavior articulates—in its own time and place—a sensibility of disenchantment that is equally viable as the visual and aural shock tactics employed by the original punk generation of the late 1970s. Collectively, the respective accounts of John, Simon, and Jo could be seen to embody strongly ingrained cultural and aesthetic sensibilities. These feelings are inherently bound up with generational remembrances of particular eras as defining moments in the development of popular music history and its associated cultural sensibilities. Indeed, as Stu, a male English punk in his mid-forties, commented while recollecting his own experience of being a teenage punk in 1977: "I feel, [well] not sorry, but I feel other people who haven't been through such a period, have missed out in a sense . . . haven't had that experience [of] being sixteen, y'know, [when] this huge thing happened."

Many interviewees perceived a palpable gap between the music and associated culture of their own youth and those of contemporary equivalents. Their exposure as teenagers to the music of the 1960s and 1970s, they claimed, had constituted a life-affirming event—and something that had affected their outlook on society and the world at large in very real and lasting ways. Music's capacity to act on contemporary youth in such a way, it was argued, had been eroded. Reasons for subscribing to this view varied among interviewees but often pointed to contemporary music's allegedly retro or recycled nature and the normalization of music through its steady absorption into broader mediascapes, such as music television, mobile phone, and information technology.

Subcultural "Forefathers"

Sentiments such as those expressed here often engendered feelings of cultural authority and ownership among aging fans regarding the popular musics they culturally invested in, the scenes they belonged to, and the relationships they formed with younger members of these scenes. An interesting example of this was seen in relation to ska punk performances I attended in the East Kent region of southeast England (see also Bennett 2006b). Originating in the early 1990s as a continuation of the reggae-punk crossover of bands such as the Clash, and also harking back to the close relationship of ska/two-tone and new wave during the late 1970s (Hebdige 1987), ska punk quickly established itself as a new underground musical style. Initially emerging in the United States, with groups such as Rancid and Operation Ivy, ska punk rapidly became a translocal scene, with groups undertaking low-key, low-budget tours across the United States and Europe. Although attracting a primarily teenage audience, ska punk has also proved to be a draw for aging punk fans. According to a number of the aging punks I interviewed, ska punk's emphasis on low-key, accessible performances, with band and audience crushed together in small, local venues, resonated with their sense of how punk "should be." There was a shared feeling among aging punks that, with the emergence of ska punk together with some of the more recent hardcore strains, punk had effectively gone back to its roots—to a cultural and performative aesthetic that they felt comfortable with and that reminded them of the "old days of true punk."

Significantly, however, when aging punks discussed their continuing attachment and loyalty to the scene, it was clear that they were viewing this attachment through a specifically altered lens. This perspective facilitated their presence among a crowd of people who were in most cases fifteen to twenty years their junior, and in some cases more junior still. Aging punks legitimated their continuing attachment to the scene in two ways. First, they occupied a particular space in the venue, away from the immediate stage area where the younger punks moshed, yet still within the main body of the crowd. From the point of view of the aging punks I interviewed, their age and accumulated experience of the punk scene supplied the license to maintain a privileged space in the venue setting. They were simultaneously at one with the crowd, yet honorably discharged from the excesses of the mosh pit, which they regarded as the domain of the young, "up-and-coming" members of the punk scene. As Mat, a punk in his late thirties, observed: "I'm gettin' old enough to . . . to let the next generation come through, y'know. It does get difficult now to go to gigs and stay at the front all the time, an' rock around all the time. I . . . I can't do it no more. [My] body's sayin', 'It's time to slow down . . . you've 'ad your fun.'"

This practice of "sticking in the back," as one interviewee put it, offers another significant insight into how older punks articulate their attachment to the punk scene. By distancing themselves from the stage and dancing area in this way, the older punks were viewing the whole event, and not just the musical performance, as the "spectacle." This sense of having an overview of a scene they believed themselves to have been instrumental in creating appeared to facilitate a self-ascribed status as subcultural "forefathers," something that was evident in the way that punks gestured to each other while watching the antics of the younger members of the audience. Indeed, on occasion, this sense of being "elders" of the punk scene manifested itself in a distinctly paternal, often protective, sense. Thus, as Jim, a punk in his late forties, observed: "It's amazin'. When the kids [younger punks] leave this place [a local music venue] to go home on a night, there's always trendies waitin' outside to slag 'em off 'cause of how they look. An' I think, 'How pathetic. Ain't they got anything better to do?'"

The second situating strategy used by the older punks was articulated through a form of discursive practice whereby they positioned themselves as critical overseers of the punk scene. This discursive practice was designed both to celebrate the survival and development of the punk scene and to self-assert the older punks' collective authority, won through age and longevity of commitment to punk, to supply critical judgment on the scene and those involved in it. This double take on the punk scene resulted in a significant juxtaposition of sentiments in the comments of older punks. They simultaneously asserted their own status as older, and thus more experienced, punks in relation to younger members of the scene and acknowledged the ways in which the younger punks were beginning to establish a legitimate punk status on their own terms. As Ron, a punk in his late forties, noted:

> It's good to see [that punk is] developing and that new people are coming along. Some of the new bands sound quite poppy really. Like this lot [pointing to flyer of a local band on the table in between us]. I don't like 'em really; they just sound

really poppy and commercial. They can all play mind you. It's like, I wish we'd had back then what they've got now. They write proper songs. All of their songs 'ave got proper beginnings, endings, and, what's it called, middle eights and stuff.

Relations between older and younger members of the punk scene also manifested themselves through "in-scene" exchanges of knowledge. Older punks I interviewed noted on several occasions how they had assumed the role of informal educators, filling in the gaps in younger punks' knowledge of the British punk scene's early years. They provided anecdotal accounts, for example, of having attended legendary performances by groups such as the Sex Pistols and handed down their personal canon of "quintessential" punk music to younger fans. In this sense, older punks saw themselves as playing an important part in preserving the punk aesthetic and passing this on to the next generation. This aspect of the intergenerational discourse among punks is effectively illustrated in the following conversation with Jezz, a punk in his late thirties:

A.B.: Do you think there's any kind of informal education going on?

Jezz: Oh, yeah, there is. Yeah, there's a girl in the village who I'm trying to get into all the stuff I'm into an' move on a bit from there, y'know. Quite good, y'know, next generation comin' through.

Indeed, the importance of older punks as conveyors of both aesthetic and practical knowledge about the punk scene was often similarly acknowledged by younger punks themselves. Rather than adopting a confrontational stance toward older members of the scene, punks in their teens and early twenties often exhibited a highly reverential attitude toward them. As Andrew, a punk in his late teens, observed:

Yeah, I think people have probably grown up with it, an' some people decide to stay with it all the way through. . . . You do see people, y'know, you can tell were punks in their youth, just like, y'know, just checking things out. Y' start chatting 'em all, y'know, an' you find out they were there [the] first time round in the '70s. An' it's quite nice to chat to 'em about that.

In many respects then, the continuing presence of aging punks in the scene is considered important by both young and old alike. As the preceding observation demonstrates, some younger punks considered older punks important role models—a view that is clearly shared by older punks, albeit for different reasons. These reasons are inherently linked with a deeply rooted, personal investment in the preservation of punk. There are interesting parallels here with Haenfler's work on the U.S. straight edge (sXe) scene. Thus, as Haenfler observes:

> For many older sXers, setting a positive example for younger kids is an important part of their ongoing commitment to sXe. They remember looking up to older members of the scene, respecting those that stayed true to sXe and feeling let down by those who left the lifestyle behind. They continue claiming sXe in part to remain true to their world. Straight edge, often framed as an "oath", "promise", or "pledge", implies that leaving the scene is a personal failure; many sXers do not want to leave this example for others to follow. (2006: 165)

Like punk, straight edge is inscribed with a series of sociocultural sensibilities that extend beyond issues of musical taste and stylistic affiliation. Its emphasis on healthy living involves a rejection of perceived social vices such as drugs, alcohol, and sexual promiscuity (see also Wood 1999, 2003). As Haenfler notes, older straight edge fans often considered displays of their ongoing commitment to such values to be a crucial aspect of their self-assumed mentoring role in relation to their younger peers.

As self-elected role models, older members of particular music scenes often come to regard such mentoring and education as an integrated aspect of their lifestyle politics. Such sensibilities are often given added gravitas because of a common perception among older scene members that the lives of their younger peers are being engulfed by an all-embracing state of anomie. They perceive that such a state has been brought on by an estrangement from mainstream politics and other dominant social institutions. Thus, as Simon, a male English dance music fan in his mid-forties, explained:

> I have this theory that the current generations are rudderless, because they have no sensible role models anymore in terms of what they want and how they want to achieve it. And when they bump into older people who share their values, they kind of grip onto them because they think, "Hey, look, I want to be doing this in twenty years time too!"

In addition to such notions of mentorship and paternalism, aging members of particular music scenes talked about other ways in which they endeavored to establish meaningful relations with younger scene members. For example, in the case of dance music, older scene members emphasized the practical skills involved in successfully running dance music events and the importance of handing this expertise down to the upcoming generation of scene members. This was clearly in evidence among older members of a dance party collective I interviewed. They expressed the shared sentiment that being older meant having a more realistic perception of the sheer levels of commitment needed to organize dance parties and to run them successfully as risk-free environments. Coordinated teamwork, it was argued, was crucial in this respect. Tasks such as putting up the marquee, or tent, assembling the public address rig, and selling drinks were regarded of equal importance in the smooth running of dance party events. Also valued was having on hand people with other skills, such as first-aid and nursing training, to help out if the need arose. This practical and responsible approach to the organization of dance party events was considered highly valuable experience for younger people who wished to become involved in the dance music scene. This attitude is evidenced in the following extract from an interview with Neil, a member of the collective in his mid-forties who both organized dance parties and acted as a DJ at party events:

A.B.: Being in your forties, do you think you have a different relationship to the dance music scene than you had earlier?

Neil: Yeah, totally. A sort of more paternal attitude to it really, I think. An' as a sort of opportunity giver as well. 'Cause I've got a marquee and a rig and contacts. An' I sort parties out an' then draw these other people in. Particularly younger people. 'Cause at the [free] parties we all stayed the same age and I quite like that big, wide age difference on the dance floor, y'know. An' to keep it inclusive really. That's what I'm after really.

A.B.: So more people can become involved in it?

Neil: Yeah. But nobody wants to, sort of, drive the van, or look after the generator or put the marquee up. Everyone wants to be a DJ. I do like to encourage new DJs, but I just say, "Oh, come along with us, we're meeting at this point, an' we're gonna put a party on." An' just drag them along with us for the whole day with all the setup.

This account again provides an interesting perspective on the way in which aging members of particular scenes seek to position themselves within these scenes, using age and experience as legitimating strategies. Describing himself essentially as a mentor, Neil goes on to relate his practice of "teaching" the tricks of the trade to young dance music enthusiasts. At many levels, this echoes the description a tradesperson might provide of his relationship with a young apprentice.

"Dad House"

Despite the affinity among old and young fans reported by some interviewees, other accounts revealed that tensions and conflicts *did* sometimes occur between different generational factions within certain music scenes. In some cases, such conflicts centered on the inscription of age-related biases in particular subgenres of music. This is evident, for example, in a further extract from my interview with Neil, the dance party organizer and DJ discussed previously. Focusing on his role as a dance music DJ, Neil said the following:

A.B.: How do you find that younger dancers and DJs respond to you? How do they see you?

Neil: "Oh, God, is he still around?" [laughs]. Eh, favorably and negatively, sometimes.

A.B.: Do some of them think you're out of touch with things?

Neil: Well, yeah, because the house music we play, which is "deep house," they call it "dad house." An' they call it that because that's the music their dads listen to. An' they tend to be into more faster musics, like hard house and techno or drum 'n' bass. . . . Our music's a bit slower tempo. It goes about one-two-four to one-two-eight beats per minute.[2]

These comments were echoed by Rick, another DJ and event organizer in his late forties, who observed: "Older people are attracted to the kind of nights I do because it's not just about BPM. There's a social aspect too. A lot of the music I play [primarily deep house] is about creating an atmosphere and chilling out."

Such observations reflect a growing trend in the dance club and party scene toward catering to an older clientele. Like older rock and pop performers whose careers began in the 1960s and 1970s (see Chapter 1), a number of dance music DJs who emerged from the house and techno scenes of the late 1980s and early 1990 have retained their original audiences and continue to play music suited to that audience's tastes. (Examples of such DJs include Carl Cox, Danny Rampling, and Fatboy Slim.)

Some aging punks also reported age-related tensions between themselves and younger punks. Like Neil, a number of aging punks identified generationally marked differences in musical taste as a key cause of conflict. Others suggested that even when punk events did attract a multigenerational following, conflicting conventions of "acceptable" crowd behavior at concerts and festivals could create their own tensions. In the decades since the original 1970s U.K. punk movement, new practices of band-audience interaction have come into being, notably stage diving (where individual fans climb on to the

---

2. Beats per minute, or BPM, is a reference to the measurement of speed or tempo in music. While, as the interviewee points out, deep house is usually around 128 BPM, more recent dance music styles tend to be faster. Jungle music, for example, is typically between 160 and 185 BPM, while speedcore and gabber exceed 200 BPM.

stage and leap off to be caught by other members of the crowd) and crowd surfing (where individuals are lifted above other members of the audience and lie on their backs to be moved across a sea of hands as if they were floating on water). Both of these practices fall outside the conventions of acceptable crowd behavior observed by many older punks. In the following extract from an interview with Phil, an English punk in his mid-forties, he discusses the generational dynamics of crowd behavior at punk festivals:[3]

A.B.: How does that work out [at punk festivals]? You've got people in their forties and fifties who are into the old-school punk and younger people who are into the new bands. What's the interaction like?

Phil: I think sometimes . . . when you do get that interaction, you've got a young crowd who are all fired up and geed up, an' they're into crowd surfin' an' things like that. So they're rollin' around on people's shoulders, an' jumpin' offstage. Now that doesn't always go down well with the old forty-somethin' punks. . . . They're not into that. They wanta just stand there and watch their favorite band. An' that can be quite annoyin', [to] have someone's size-nine [boot] whop you on the back o' the head as they're rollin' around crowd surfin'. So, the odd thing happens, y'know, you might get the odd ding-dong where the two age groups clash, ehm, purely because it's a sort of modern method o' dancin', ehm, an' it doesn't go down very well.

This account points to a significant aesthetic rift between young and old punks related to their differing generational attachments to punk and the way these attachments indicate different ways of "being punk" and engaging with the music. While older punks may sometimes "pogo dance"[4] at punk events, many simply stand, watch the

---

3. Punk festivals, which have become increasingly popular since the 1990s, typically feature a mixture of old and newer punk acts from the international punk scene.

4. This is the name given to a form of punk dance common during the late 1970s in which individuals jump up and down on the spot as if riding a pogo stick.

band, and enjoy the music. For younger punks, attendance at a punk gig typically involves the embodied enjoyment and appreciation of the music (Thomas 2003) in more visually spectacular and physically testing ways, as manifested through stage diving and crowd surfing. As Breen (1991) and Tsitsos (1999) observe, such contemporary forms of crowd behavior, although ostensibly appearing random and reckless in nature, do in fact embody distinctive codes of collectivity and togetherness. These codes are based, in part, on a need for group coordination in order for such potentially physically dangerous activities to be conducted successfully and safely. However, as the extract from my interview with Phil illustrates, such codes of crowd behavior are not necessarily understood, or appreciated, by older punks, whose appreciation of the music, sense of association with the crowd, and acquired reading of acceptable crowd conventions are often qualitatively different.

Age No Object? Multigenerational Rock and Pop Bands

The foregoing examples illustrate the tensions that can arise in multigenerational music scenes as a result of conflicting, age-related forms of behavior. An interesting exception here was in the field of musicmaking. Although it was not a central topic of my research, as previously observed, a number of interviewees did make music and play in bands, and in some cases these bands had multigenerational lineups. Traditionally speaking, the rock or pop group has been a site of practice heavily circumscribed by age. As recently as the mid-1990s, research on music-making depicted this as a youth-dominated field in which forms of identity work, resistance, and escapism could be enacted (Fornäs, Lindberg, and Sernhade 1995). In her work on local music-making practices in Liverpool, Cohen (1991) similarly notes how the music scene was segregated by age, with younger musicians playing original material, written with a view to securing a recording contract, while older musicians tended to resign themselves to playing in pub bands, whose repertoire typically comprised cover versions of rock and pop standards from the 1950s onward.

On the basis of the research conducted for this book, such age-related divisions in music-making practices would appear to be dissolving, with multigenerational bands being far more common than they may have been fifteen to twenty years ago. A number of factors may contribute to this change. To begin with, the practice of music-making is becoming more diverse, with the once dominant guitar/bass/drums band format now merely one aspect of the music-making field. The field also encompasses, for example, turntabling, sampling, and a range of other studio-based forms of music-making engaged in by people with little or no interest in mastering a conventional rock instrument or, in some cases, giving live performances of their work. Within this shifting context, young people with a desire to pursue more "traditional" forms of music-making may find a greater range of opportunities to do so if they are willing to work with older musicians, for whom guitar/bass/drum combos are still typically a more dominant mode of music-making practice. Similarly, it is fair to say that the field of professional rock and pop music-making is not nearly as circumscribed by images of youthfulness as it once was. As noted in Chapter 1, rock icons such as Paul McCartney, Bob Dylan, and the Rolling Stones, now well into their sixties and beyond, continue to tour and record new material. Similarly, even those artists associated with the punk and new wave backlash against the aging 1970s rock aristocracy—for example, the Sex Pistols, U2, and R.E.M.—are now in their fifties. The widened acceptance of aging as a normal aspect of performing rock musicians' careers, and as something that may indeed add dimensions of artistic richness and creativity to their music, has in many respects supplanted the earlier view that rock music was a youth form—performed by the young for the young (see Bennett 2008a).

This new perception of rock and pop as uni-age fields of musical practice appears to permeate all levels of music-making, right down to the local/informal level. This is evident not only in the growing number of multigenerational rock and pop bands observed in local scenes but also through the non-ageist sensibilities that appear to inform such bands and their creative pursuits. For example, Steven, a British-born tradesperson, amateur musician, and singer in his late

forties who lives in Australia, recalled how he gained contact with the
fellow musicians in his current band:

> I answered a few ads. Y'know, like in the paper and in music
> shops [where] people put up cards an' that. And you select
> cards of, y'know, music that you might be interested in play-
> ing. . . . I phoned this bloke. And what [had] attracted me
> to his advert was [that] he said "Britpop"—Oasis, Blur, etc.
> An' I thought, "That sounds interesting, sounds better than
> AC/DC covers!" So [I] phoned him up an' he didn't ask that
> question [about age]. So, I said at the end [of our conversa-
> tion], "Okay, we'll arrange to get together an' have a jam, an'
> does it matter how old I am?" An' he said, "No, of course it
> doesn't. I don't care how old you are!" All right, fine. So, eh,
> we met up. He was nineteen, or eighteen even. I was thirty-
> eight, thirty-seven, something like that. The singer, she was
> like sixteen. Y'know, very young. And, eh, the drummer, he
> was eighteen. [The] bass player, he was in his probably twen-
> ties, I suppose . . . so they were quite inexperienced musically.
> Ehm, but what they all had in common was keenness. Y'know,
> they really wanted to play. And, eh, that's all I needed, y'know,
> some people who were keen and loved it, an' wanted to play.

Similar stories were also told about young musicians who, disillusioned with the attitude of their peers, had sought out bands consisting of older musicians. These young musicians believed the older band
members were more dedicated and more apt to take music-making
seriously. Again, it was clear in such accounts that issues of age were far
less important to these young musicians than the overall quality and
satisfaction of the band experience. As Andrew, a South Australian
punk in his late forties who played drums and sang with a Ramones
tribute band, described the relationship he and Suzy, the group's guitarist, had with the band's nineteen-year-old female bass player:

> Some of [her] friends, say, y'know, "Why don't you get in a
> band with young people? What are you hangin' around with

those old farts for?" An' she's just shocked by that. And that's been the end of their friendship really 'cause she thinks, "Wow, that's so ageist and discriminatory." An', y'know, to her it's been the best thing that could happen in her life, because she wanted to play in a rock 'n' roll band. She wanted to play punk music. An', y'know, basically for a young girl tryin' to get into that, she ran into a few difficult boys an' people with bad ideas and bad attitudes an' drug problems an' those sorts of things. And to come along to us an' we're just like, full speed ahead. "Yeah, okay, you're in, we're playing on Saturday and then we're recording next month, then we're goin' overseas the month after that." She's loved it and it's been great.

As these accounts illustrate, in tandem with the increasingly uni-age profile of popular music as a global industry, a new territory of amateur and semiprofessional music-making appears to be unfolding— one in which issues of age difference between musicians are taking a backseat to shared aesthetic and creative aspirations. Older musicians are inspired by the energy and ambition of their younger peers, and younger people in turn are motivated by the commitment and experience of older band members. As Nick, the nineteen-year-old guitarist of a band led by someone twenty years his senior, observed: "It's been a steep learning curve, musically and personally. He [the band leader] won't take any crap. No missing rehearsals, no posing, no making comments about women in the crowd at gigs, y'know. What he's interested in is the music, and puttin' on a good gig."

"And the Kids Can Come Too": Festivals and Parties as Family Outings

The festival setting is another sphere of musical life that is becoming increasingly multigenerational. The inclusion of children in concert and festival-going activities is certainly not a new phenomenon. For example, the original Woodstock festival of 1969, considered by many as the catalyst for the contemporary rock festival (Laing 2004) and mythologized over the years as a politically charged event (Street 2004), was also something of a family outing for many. It was portrayed as such in the opening sequences of Michael Wadleigh's film of the event, *Woodstock* (see Bell 1999; Bennett 2004a). However, in the four decades since the original Woodstock event, the diversification of the festival scene has led to an increasingly child-friendly aesthetic among festivalgoers and organizers alike. Bloustien (2004b) describes such a scenario in her account of WOMADelaide, a biennial festival staged in the South Australian capital city of Adelaide as a local arm of WOMAD (World of Music and Dance), a concept originated by singer Peter Gabriel. Bloustien relates the established practice of letting young children sit in trees around the festival site, thus allowing them an unobstructed view of the music performances. As Bloustien notes, this practice has become an essentially ritualistic aspect of the WOMADelaide experience to the extent that it is now an accepted part of the general ambience of the event.

The relative ease with which intergenerational exchanges can and do take place in festival and party spaces, and the bonds that they create between young and old, are further illustrated in the following account by John, an Englishman in his late fifties. In describing his first trip to the annual U.K. WOMAD festival and his surprise at the diversity of ages of the crowd, John said:

> There is a lot of mixing. And I remember vividly . . . I was with a friend the same age as me. And he'd gone off and we had two chairs, fold-up chairs, 'cause we're old geezers [laughs]. And I was sitting on my [chair] and the one next to me was empty. An' this kid, who must have only been ten or twelve, came up and said, "Is anyone sitting there?" and I said, "Well, not for the moment. You're welcome to sit there until he returns." And he did, and he was so friendly, an' he was chatting away. An' [he asked], "Is this your first time at WOMAD?" an' I said yes. An' he said, "I've been coming here for five years," since he was seven or something! An' I said, "Isn't it lovely?" 'cause it was hot and sunny an' everything. "It's always sunny at WOMAD," he said! And, y'know, there was this wonderful kind of [rapport], it didn't matter that he was twelve an' I was fifty. It was wonderful. And that was really appealing, more so than the music in a way.

One obvious point to make in relation to festivals such as WOMAD, its regional equivalents, and similar events is that they have become established as spaces for a particularly middle-class celebration of musical and cultural diversity. Thus, a criticism that could be leveled against such festival spaces is that they merely uphold a middle-class code of family involvement and adult-child exchange that has long been in evidence across a broad sphere of middle-class leisure activities. At the same time, however, it is also fair to say that family festival-going activities, and the forms of parent-child inter-action they involve, are not merely restricted to festivals such as WOMAD. On the contrary, a number of musical genres/scenes that challenge bourgeois ideologies and middle-class values also exhibit an increasing tolerance toward family involvement.

A clear case in point is the annual Punk Rock Picnic staged in the London borough of Brixton. This event is also essentially multigenerational, with family groups in attendance. In the sphere of dance music too, there is an increasing tolerance of the inclusion of families and children, especially within the free party scene. The free party movement, with its origins in the free festivals of the early 1970s, quickly gathered momentum during the mid-1980s with the emergence of electronic dance music styles such as house and techno (see McKay 1996, 1998). As original members of the free party scene have aged and the scene has diversified into a number of smaller, often localized subscenes, family involvement is becoming an increasingly normal aspect of the dance party experience. This was evident in accounts offered by members of a small, close-knit dance collective based in the southeast of England. The group had something of an open-door policy regarding the inclusion of children. In addition to being a necessary organizational element in the staging of dance par-ties for and by people who wished to involve their families, this infor-mal policy of inclusivity had another benefit. It was considered highly desirable when contrasted with what was perceived to be an overtly inscribed exclusivity in more youth-centered scenes. Paul, in his early fifties and one of the principal dance party organizers, explained:

> [A lot of] youth cultures focus on a particular genre to exclude other people. Hip-hop is a classic example because it's quite

narrowly defined, [and] the hip-hop guys listen to a specific type of hip-hop and they all dress in a certain way, an' it's their scene. Whereas with ours, it's more open to anyone who wants to come along, regardless of what age you are, what clothes you're wearing, or the fact that you've got a couple of kids in tow.

Indeed, according to fellow collective member Brian, a father in his early forties, assuming the children were properly supervised, attending dance parties could be a positive learning experience for children. Thus, he observed:

You take your kids along [to dance parties]. An' I think it's a good education for them. Okay, sometimes you've got to explain stuff to them. An' sometimes people get a bit out of order, an' you've got to say "Excuse me, my kid's here, could you pack it in please?" But normally people are okay about that.

For Brian, there was no apparent contradiction between his role as a father and his interest and involvement in a local dance party scene. This was a view shared by many others involved in the collective. Having made the decision to incorporate the party scene into their lifestyle, rather than try to find ways of keeping this and their domestic concerns apart, collective members looked for ways to combine these two aspects of their lives. Moreover, it was clear from the accounts of other members of the collective that in including children in party events, they took considerable care to ensure that the experience would be a positive one for them. For example, in discussing the outdoor dance parties organized each summer by the collective, Jake, a collective member in his early sixties, provided the following account of the child-care and leisure activities built into these events:

[Children] are never left. There's always one "auntie." But, at parties, people have got tents anyway, so they'll do their bit and then go and sleep. This is it, it always works. Kids, they have the best time. Especially if we fix up a swing for them. And we organize stuff, you know, adventure walks or trips to the beach. . . . "First one to come back with a limpet shell gets a prize." That's what kids should do, y'know, enjoy being children. Sometimes we organize midnight feasts, y'know, a bit naughty. But, nobody's getting them up in the morning. So, they get up at ten o'clock or so, bit of breakfast, then off to the beach for the day.

This dance party collective's pride in its ability to organize parties that were inclusive—together with their emphasis on risk-free fun countenanced by a careful policing of drug and alcohol consumption and quick, efficient resolution of any form of antisocial behavior—was a core aspect of its collective sense of identity. Within this, it was clear that age played a significant part. Age and accumulated life experience, it was suggested, were key ingredients in their particular style of party organization and also often worked in their favor in dealing with the authorities. On several occasions, I was told of an incident in which the local police visited a party site as the collective was preparing for an event. As dance party organizer Neil described it:

The police arrived and I think they were quite surprised to see a bunch of middle-aged people. So they just told us to make sure we were packed up and gone by ten o'clock the following morning or something, and that was it. An' the following week, the local paper had this story that read something like "Middle-age ravers told to leave by ten a.m.—an' they did!"

As the dance party scene acquires longevity, it is likely that scenarios such as those described will become more common. Like the other musics thus far discussed in this book, the dance party scene is now essentially multigenerational. As such, it is open to a variety of interpretations and stagings of collective belonging and inclusion dependent upon the composition of individuals in a specific collective or group.

Building Bridges: Shared Musical Tastes among Parents and Children

A prominent theme in interviews with aging music fans, especially among those with teenage children, was the importance of music in building parent-child relationships. As noted in Chapter 1, successive new musics, notably extreme metal and various hard-core genres, may still function to split generational tastes, while the continuing attempts by organizations such as the Parents Music Resource Center (PMRC) to censor the work of some popular music artists illustrate how easily youth musics can still become the focus of a moral panic (see Martin and Segrave 1993). Such examples, however, make for a somewhat incomplete representation of popular music's significance at an intergenerational level. In her highly instructive work on older female fans of Kate Bush music (see also Chapter 2), Vroomen (2004) notes how one such fan, in her early forties, had been able to use her interest in and knowledge of various genres of popular music as a means of forging a close relationship with her stepdaughter— whose own musical tastes had grown and developed as a result of this.

Similarly, I have noted elsewhere how such a shared interest in music between parents and children has in turn given rise to extra-musical forms of association based on the experiences of listening to and talking about music together (see Bennett 2000, 2006a). The impact of music on parent-child relationships is also a growing topic in popular literature. For example, in his book *Two of Us*, Peter Smith chronicles how introducing his seven-year-old son to the music of the Beatles provided an avenue for them to talk about a variety of subjects and, in the process, brought the two of them closer together. Thus, concludes Smith: "Just as the Beatles were a portal to other music, they were a portal to a friendship between me and my son" (2004: 192).

As a dominant aspect of the soundscape in many home environments, popular music often becomes an anchoring point for early childhood memories, informing children's experience of growing up and their formative relationships with their parents (see, for example, Bennett 2000; DeNora 2000). Many interviewees reflected on this, additionally noting how their own musical tastes had provided a basis for their children's early interest in and appreciation of popular music. Steven observed: "My eldest son probably wouldn't have got into reggae if I hadn't been playing it constantly when he was young." Among parents who claimed they had provided such an early impetus for their children's musical interest, such claims often were set in the context of a subsequent maturation of their musicalized relationship and sharing of musical influences and ideas. What seemed important to those interviewed was not that their children grew up liking the artists or genres that they themselves preferred, but rather that their children acquired a good *feel* for music—and an ability to justify their musical tastes in ways that addressed issues of "cultural value" and "authenticity," subjective as these concepts were perceived to be. Indeed, many parents seemed entirely comfortable entering into critical discussions about popular music with their children and often allowing them to assume the role of tastemaker. This attitude is clearly illustrated in the following account, again from Steven:

> [My son] has introduced me to certain music that I wouldn't necessarily have, y'know, listened to, which I've ended up lovin' actually. Nirvana is a classic case. . . . [My son] bought *Nevermind* [Nirvana's breakthrough album] and, eh, more or less sat me down and said "listen to this." An' he was right, y'know. Kurt [Cobain] knew how to write a song, no two ways about it.

In other cases, such processes of music exchange and reciprocity were punctuated by debates between parents and their children. These discussions concerned the merits or not of new technologies as necessary aspects of creative engagement with musical texts. In one particular case, John, an Englishman in his mid-fifties with a preference for late 1960s rock and folk-rock music, claimed that, having initially opposed the use of "computers and technology" in music-making, he had been considerably enlightened by his teenage son's use of such facilities. Moreover, as John went on to explain, the use of his own vinyl record collection by his son as a sampling resource had fostered a new level of musicalized dialogue between the pair and led to collaboration in the creative process of music-making.

John: What I do like is that [my son] actually likes a lot of the sixties stuff . . . although of course he's, y'know, intent on sampling the sixties stuff and putting in twenty-first-century stuff.

A.B.: So do a lot of your vinyl records get used for sampling?

John: Yes, they do. Which is fine. I don't mind that too much. Eh,
I'm flattered in the way that he thinks it's worth doing. So
that's quite nice.

A.B.: Does he consult you when sampling stuff?

John: He does. And when I hear something new, or new to me,
which I think he might like, he's actually quite open and will
listen to it. So in a way I read that as him respecting my judgment. He might then turn around and say it was crap, y'know,
that's fine. Yeah, it's good. I'm actually quite refreshed . . . by
the way he's turning out musically.

Earlier in this chapter, it was noted how one interviewee, Simon,
perceived the appropriation of contemporary music styles by the
parent generation as something that created a new musical generation gap. He said it pushed children toward more "extreme" musical
styles as a means of rebelling against their parents. Interestingly, the
research for this book identified examples of parent-child exchanges
about popular music that often suggested a somewhat different scenario in play. The following account offered by Lynne, a professional
woman in her mid-forties, is an interesting case in point. Lynne
described her and her husband's acquired interest in dance music and
its impact on their son's musical taste and music-making practice:

If anything, I probably had some fairly negative views on
[dance music] because this was when my husband and I
had teenage kids. So we associated it with rave culture and,
y'know, "dangerous drugs" and things that we didn't really
have any grip on. So, [initially clubbing] was really more of
just a social scene, y'know, with the local people going to clubs
and things like that, so that was how we got to know the music
originally. And then . . . I think it was in 1998, some friends of
ours took us to a club in Brixton, which, at the time, was kind
of, I suppose, part of the underground dance scene that was

going on in the southeast of London. And [that] one night in a club completely altered our mindsets. It just changed us completely really, frankly, And, eh, y'know, you get a bit evangelical about it really, and all your friends have got to go.

As the preceding account reveals, Lynne and her husband were initially apprehensive about dance music, primarily because of its potentially negative effects on their children if they were exposed to it. However, through their own absorption in the clubbing scene, the couple subsequently revised their views. Indeed, this change of heart extended to actively encouraging their son's interest in dance music and involvement in the scene as a DJ. Thus, as Lynne observed:

Our son, who's now twenty-one, I think we had quite a big influence in his interest in dance music, and his choice of dance music, and what he's now into. He's got into deejaying and doing his own parties and things like that. And I think it would be true to say that that really came from us, from what we were interested in doing, the music and the clubs that we went to. And from our parties. Our son deejayed-out at the parties that we did.

When asked about her other children, and whether they too had become interested in dance music, Lynne gave an equally interesting response. In contrast to her son, whose embrace of the dance music scene resonated with Lynne's own acquired feelings toward dance music, her daughter, she felt, led a rather more conservative lifestyle, this being punctuated by her musical tastes and nighttime leisure preferences:

My youngest daughter, who's nineteen now, she's always been into more kind of soul-based funky music, and not really . . . I mean she goes out to local clubs with her friends. But she's not into clubbing in any serious kind of way. For her, it's more about going out to a local night with a few friends, having a few drinks, and, you know, coming home about one o'clock in the morning.

Such a depiction is significant in that it suggests an interesting deconstruction of the once clearly delineated generation gap existing between parents and children and the role of music in relation to this. Lynne's portrayal of her daughter would suggest that the accusations of conservatism once directed at parents by their children through the expressive platform of musical taste may just as easily be inverted in an age where parents are as likely as their children to opt for particular musical genres and associated lifestyle practices.

On other occasions, interviewee accounts of the musicalized relationships they enjoyed with their children were punctuated by biographical commonalities they perceived between themselves and their pop/rock icons, commonalities that sometimes also took into account such icons' own parent-child relationships. Thus, for example, François, a middle-aged graphic artist from northern France, explained how a preference for the British progressive rock band Genesis as a teenager had led him to follow the post-Genesis career of original singer Peter Gabriel. As Gabriel had become more influenced by non-Western musical styles, so too did François's tastes broaden in that direction. They also became a focus for musical exchanges with his teenage daughter, who had, in turn, introduced her father to rap music. In articulating his identity as a middle-aged father with a daughter who had, in his view, acquired his keen passion for music, François likened himself to Gabriel:

> I love the way Peter Gabriel has evolved as an artist. I'm about the same age as him. I am fifty-two and I think that Peter Gabriel is fifty-six. Physically, he had long hair too [when he was younger]. He crowd surfed when he was twenty years old. . . . Now, he is like me [he points to his short, thinning hair]. He is calm. During his last gig, his daughter sang with him. And I have daughters [too]. He loves world music, and I think he has a certain point of view on the world, which is the one that I have too.[5]

---

5. Interview was originally conducted in French with assistance from Hervé Glevarec. English translation was provided by Hervé Glevarec.

The preceding account provides a further illustration of how the baby-boomer icons of the 1960s and early 1970s continue to act as role models in the lives of their aging popular music audiences. In Chapter 1, it was suggested that such a continuing role model function also extends to the construction and management of an aging body and identity. In the aforementioned case, we are presented with a compelling example of how an aging music fan's lifestyle, including his musically informed relationship with his children, is based on a continuing identification with Peter Gabriel as both fan and icon have aged together. In this sense, Gabriel's biographical development as an aging popular music icon with a generationally imbued sense of cultural significance is relevant. It provides a series of critical benchmarks for François in the construction and management of his own aging identity.

The significance of popular music as a multigenerational resource in contemporary society manifests itself in a variety of ways. As this chapter has illustrated, any attempt to read age-based relationships between music fans in an essentialist way quickly breaks down, given the multiple sensibilities at play. Certainly, on one level, aging popular music fans can be seen to harbor particular understandings of themselves as in some way superior to their younger peers, considering their generational attachment to the origins and critical historical moments of specific music scenes. In other cases, the dynamics of aging fans' interactions with their younger peers engender sensibilities of eldership and paternalism. However, multigenerational musical worlds may also facilitate collaboration and communication between the generations, as seen, for example, in relation to local multigenerational rock bands and the music-informed dialogues and exchanges that occur between parents and their children.

6 / Still "Changing the World"?

Music, Aging, and Politics

I think . . . [from] '76 to '79 there was like a little window, a little
tear in the fabric of reality. An' like thousands of people fell
through it, then it closed up. An' sort of like, we can't get back even
if we wanted to. I do see that, an' I reckon a similar thing happened
in the sixties as well, between say '64 an' '69. Y'know, a lot of
people never came back, or could go back from that experience.
(Chris, an English punk, aged forty-four)

The previous chapters in this book have all considered, in various ways, the long-term influence of popular music on the lives of aging fans. One issue not yet examined, but clearly worthy of discussion, is the impact of music on the political values of aging popular music fans. The relationship between popular music and politics has been a regular topic of discussion since the early 1970s, when a series of books, among them Reich's *The Greening of America* (1971) and Denisoff and Peterson's edited volume *The Sounds of Social Change* (1972), considered how popular music had served as a platform for various political issues from the 1950s onward. The debate continued into the 1980s and 1990s, with, for example, Frith's (1981; 1983) work on the cultural representation of rock as a cornerstone of the establishment of an alternative "ideological" community by the hippie counterculture and, in the 1990s, Garofalo's (1992) analysis of music's role in raising awareness of social issues through mega-events such as Live Aid, and McKay's (1996) study of the DIY politics central to the anarcho-punk and free party movements.

As some of this work has sought to illustrate, much of the political rhetoric espoused by popular music artists and their audiences has often been fundamentally flawed. These flaws result from the overly idealistic and, in many cases, inherently naive claims that have been made about the capacity of music to effect social change. Thus, for example, Frith (1981, 1983) argues that a key problem with the counterculture's belief in the significance of rock music as the basis for an alternative "community" was the highly romanticized notion implicit in such a belief regarding music's capacity for bringing about social change. As Frith goes on to explain, rock music itself could offer no material basis, or set of political tools, in which to ground such an alternative community. Similarly, Garofalo (1992) points to the inherent shortcomings in the philosophy underpinning Live Aid and the other consciousness-raising mega-events of the 1980s and early 1990s. As Garofalo observes, in the context of mega-events, popular music itself was no longer considered to be a tool for effecting sociopolitical change; rather, music was used as a means of drawing a large number of people together to generate financial aid and raise awareness of a specific issue, such as Third World famine or political oppression.

Given the stated shortcomings of popular music as a purveyor of political messages and action, one is left to ponder the political legacy of particular chapters in post–Second World War popular music history, such as the counterculture and punk. In the context of such a debate, the voices of those who were involved in these movements are of special importance. Indeed, generally speaking, retrospective accounts of the political dimensions of hippie, punk, and other music-related scenes and movements tend to rely on populist interpretations supplied by journalists, musicians, and others in the media spotlight. As this chapter will illustrate, however, accounts by ordinary people, that is to say, those with little or nothing at stake in the popular representation of hippie, punk, and so on, often reveal a far more nuanced and personalized history of the relationship between popular music and politics. Moreover, as the following accounts suggest, age often brings with it an enhanced level of personal reflection. In discussing the political and spiritual aspirations garnered through involvement with hippie and punk philosophies, many interviewees talk less about a distinctly youth-based experience—a temporal radicalism subsumed by the pressures and expectations of adulthood—than an ongoing development in their worldview, in which a political awareness acquired during youth has continued to grow and mature.

If You Can Remember the Sixties . . .

> We tend to forget this, that the lives of the vast majority of people were simply untouched by the so-called spirit of the sixties; that most people went through most of the decade hardly knowing what a hippie was, still less interested in what hippies had to say. (Stone 1999: 21)

In this quote from his semi-autobiographical book *The Last of the Hippies*, author C. J. Stone laments the extent to which the 1960s as a decade, and the hippie movement as a pinnacle of that decade's allegedly radical stance, have been mythologized over the years. In Stone's view, much of the everyday reality of the 1960s has simply been airbrushed out of existence. The 1960s, according to Stone, have taken on a preferred, inherently populist meaning. A similar view is expressed by Street (2004) in an essay on the political myths associated with the original 1969 Woodstock festival. According to Street, the key significance of the Woodstock festival today centers largely on its place in popular memory as a symbolic metaphor for the countercultural movement as a utopian moment in late-twentieth-century history. This populist view conveniently overlooks the rapid demise of the countercultural project in the wake of Woodstock—a product of both the counterculture's inherent naïveté concerning its ability to install radical social change and the rapid commodification of the hippie lifestyle (see, for example, Palmer 1976).

The perceived flaws in the countercultural project, including the hypocrisy associated with some of the anticapitalist messages communicated by particular countercultural icons, have produced an air of ambivalence that still hangs over the memory of the 1960s. The specter of the "old hippie" clutching the dream of a new utopian society has been cited numerous times as a key motivation for the rise of punk in the late 1970s; it has also become a popular stereotype in situation comedy and satire, an obvious example being the character Neil in the early 1980s British television series *The Young Ones* (Bannister 2006). The fact that many of those who "dropped out" during the 1960s—that is, left their jobs and university courses to join communes or travel on the "hippie trail" to places such as Morocco and India— simply dropped back in to relatively comfortable, middle-class life-styles and careers was still further cause for consternation among subsequent youth cultures. The youth cultures that came after the hippie movement viewed the actions of those who dropped back in as little more than a sham—a pretense of radical politicized action that wholly lacked coherence and collective commitment.

In conducting the research for this book, I was therefore especially interested in locating and talking to old hippies and those formerly associated with the hippie movement about their memories of living through the late 1960s and early 1970s. I also wanted to know how they felt this experience had shaped them politically. As I began the interviews, a common picture quickly began to emerge. Those individuals who described themselves as old hippies, or claimed a former allegiance to hippie values, typically offered mixed accounts of how an association with the counterculture had impacted their subsequent adult lives. Such accounts were at once critical of much of the hippie rhetoric but at the same time confident that this experience had influenced personal lifestyle, outlook, and political views in fundamental, long-term, and, on the whole, positive ways. Several interviewees were quite dismissive of what they now considered to be the superficial radicalism of their "hippie" youth. For these individuals, the progression of time and the tempering that comes with the aging process had effected a critical distance from particular aspects of the hippie milieu. Similarly, time and ageing had engendered a more self-reflective and philosophical interpretation of hippie culture, its place in the everyday culture of the 1960s, and its subsequent impact on the interviewees as individuals and on the cultural fabric of society as a whole.

From the 1950s onward, technological developments in the mediation and consumption of music increasingly facilitated its use among youth audiences in their stylistic and ideological practice (Melly 1970; Chambers 1985; Shumway 1992). The late 1960s counterculture marks an important progression in this trend. During the late 1960s, popular music became increasingly radical and "countercultural" in its content and style (Bennett 2001a). This change was heard both in popular music lyrics—which, following the lead of early 1960s folk-revival artist Bob Dylan, became critically concerned with issues of inequality, oppression, and other forms of social injustice (Billig 2000)—and in the music itself. Both established artists, such as the Beatles and the Rolling Stones, and a newer generation of artists, including the Grateful Dead, the Doors, and Jimi Hendrix, began producing music of a more experimental and, in some cases, avant-garde nature. These and other artists were considered pioneers of a new, more artistic and intellectual sphere of popular music that became crystallized through "rock"—a term that, although not new, increasingly came to be used as a means of demarcating "serious" music from chart-oriented popular music from the mid-1960s onward (Bennett 2007). The compositional and lyrical departures that characterized rock had significant implications for both its production and reception. Thus, as Harron (1990) observes, record companies were initially unsure how to market much of the new countercultural rock music being produced and consequently were forced to recruit young "street-wise" hippies to advise them. At a cultural level, the hippies' investment in rock went further than a mere aesthetic interest in its music and lyrics; music was considered a new form of political voice and the bedrock of a countercultural community (Frith 1981, 1983). This aspect of rock's purported place in hippie ideology is famously documented in Michael Wadleigh's film *Woodstock*. When festival organizer Michael Lang is asked to explain the significance of music for the youth audience, Lang replies obliquely that effectively the *message* is in the music itself (see Bell 1999).

Returning to the subject of countercultural music at a distance of some forty years, the observations of the ageing hippies interviewed for this book were instructive. For some, the discussion of countercultural music was framed within a discourse of rapid social, cultural, and technological change occurring in the 1960s that acted as a springboard for the impact of music on the collective consciousness of youth at that time. Thus, John, an Englishman in his late fifties, recalled his experience of watching the Beatles' televised performance of their song "All You Need Is Love" in June 1967:[1]

> I remember very well, the night [when] the Beatles broadcast "All You Need Is Love" around the world. And whilst I was never a Beatles fan, [although] I was obviously very much aware of them, that was quite a special night. Partly because it was very much a hippie song, but also because it had such a universal coverage and it was just amazing. . . . I'm not sure whether [the music] actually did anything. I think at the time we thought it was doing something. Because it was reaching out, because it had such a wide reach.

For John, countercultural music remains locked within a particular time and place in which it has become symbolically enshrined, not because of any particular legacy but because of the emotive energy and belief that John and those around him invested in music and the potential of music during the late 1960s. Moreover, there is in John's account a strong sense of affectivity, that is, an assumed bond with others who might have shared the globally mediated experience of watching the Beatles' performance. Indeed, later during the interview, John returned to this topic, suggesting that the Beatles' performance of "All You Need Is Love" affectively bonded members of his generation through both their shared memory of the event and its impact on their sense of generational belonging—one distinctly tied to a coming of age during the time of the countercultural movement.

Other interviewees displayed a far more critical view of the counterculture and were at pains to point out the hypocrisy that they had over time come to identify as a fatal flaw in the ideology underpinning the political rock music of the late 1960s. Rock music, they felt, became essentially fetishized by a woefully misguided hippie youth

---

1. Although subsequently released as a single (in July 1967), "All You Need Is Love" was first performed live by the Beatles as part of the *Our World* program, the world's first live global television linkup. The program was broadcast via satellite on June 25, 1967, and was viewed by an estimated 400 million people in twenty-six countries.

who invested an element of belief in the subversive qualities of rock that, even during the 1960s, was clearly unjustified. This view is clearly expressed in the following account from Mike, an Englishman in his mid-fifties and a self-professed "old hippie":

> [Music] was a carrier of a kind of new message. . . . I mean to us it was that rock music was going to change the world. Y'know, what I mean, we actually thought that. Eh, an' it was the carrier of a whole kind of spirit really, to do with youth, to do with rebellion, to do with change. . . . Ehm, the bands were part of it, because they expressed something. I mean it gets a bit ironic when you look back on it and think that, eh, the Rolling Stones did a song called "Street Fighting Man," yeah, y'know, eh, which is all about political revolution. . . . An', y'know, there's a sort of irony in that. It's a kind of facade of rebellion rather than actual rebellion.

Such responses were quite common among interviewees who had self-identified as hippies during the late 1960s. With the benefit of nearly four decades of hindsight, many felt that the hippie ideology was inherently naive and that a key factor in this naïveté was the unerring faith in the power of music to bring about social and cultural change. In addressing this issue, a number of interviewees offered critical dissections of song lyrics that were once deemed central to the transmission of the countercultural message. Many claimed to now find the lyrics of some of the counterculture's most prominent artists naive and immature. Dave, a former hippie from southeast England and now a schoolteacher in his late fifties, talked about what he now perceived as the "quite thin rock poetry" of the late 1960s and the counterculture:

> It comes as quite a surprise to listen to a lot of that music now. At the times the lyrics seemed so, I suppose, vital. A lot of it now seems pretty hollow. But I guess that's part of the thing about growing up and looking for something that seems edgy, at least in relation to your life experience at that point.

A similar opinion was offered by Mike, who observed:

> Listening to Jim Morrison's[2] lyrics now, I mean they're pretty naff [uncool]. Yeah, all right, this guy, y'know, it's early kind of environmentalism and stuff, in some ways. But some of it's really naff, y'know. Wanting to hear a butterfly scream? Well, y'know. What? It's a nonsense!

According to a number of interviewees, their solution to the problems they identified with countercultural rock had been to abandon the counterculture altogether, a decision preempted in some cases by the decline of the counterculture itself at the end of the 1960s. During the intervening decades, several interviewees claimed to have engaged with a variety of successive scenes—punk during the late 1970s, the free party scene of the mid-1980s, and the rave scene of the late 1980s and early 1990s. Although, anecdotally, political connections between the hippie, punk, and dance music scenes are often expressed[3] in terms of their academic representation, these scenes typically are depicted as culturally and historically distinct. A notable exception here is found in McKay's work (1996), which identifies a political thread running through and linking the more radical elements of a number of scenes, from hippie, through punk, to the free party scene and beyond. Interestingly, McKay's observed mobility of political ideologies through these scenes was to some extent substantiated by several of my own interviewees.

This is evident in the following account from Susan, a fifty-seven-year-old Englishwoman now working in the nonprofit volunteer sector.

---

2. Jim Morrison was lead vocalist and lyricist for the U.S. countercultural rock group the Doors in the 1960s. Following his death in 1971 at the age of twenty-seven, Morrison, and the Doors, acquired a cult status, which has endured ever since. Renowned for his introspective and often allegorical lyrics, Morrison is regarded by many as an early example of a rock poet, alongside artists such as Bob Dylan.

3. Most dramatically, in my own research, in a middle-aged clubber's description of his participation in an underground dance music scene in London and confrontation with, as he put it, "Fifty-five [to] sixty-year-old acid casualties, sort of with their faces painted, going Arggg!"

The hippie thing, or counterculture, whatever you want to call it, did burn itself out quite quickly. I think from the start a lot of people quickly got the idea it couldn't go on forever, maybe not for much longer. And people always think that, you know, "once a hippie," kind of thing. But I actually got quite involved in the politics of punk, when it came along. For me, some of the harder-edge legacy of hippie resurfaced in punk.

Mike took a similar view, as revealed in the charting of his own transition from countercultural rock to punk and the reasons underpinning this transition:

The problem with the kind of music we were listening to was that it was very [much] like we were—it had an overblown view of itself. It thought it was something kind of really important. Eh, it was like, y'know, people were comparing *Sergeant Pepper*[4] to Mozart, things like this. You had all these concept albums coming out. . . . An' when punk came in, it just came in on a completely different angle. Y'know, gettin' back to basics, simple numbers, fast, exciting again, and with an edge and not so up its own arse as it were. So that really changed things for me, I just really took to the punk bands, y'know.

The way in which Mike describes his transition from hippie to punk music is significant in that it belies both an evolving and a shifting perception of music as a platform for ideological practice and belief. Indeed, as Mike elaborated on in these above comments, he explained how his understanding of and response to music began to change. In his countercultural years, Mike had perceived the music in itself as an important statement on culture and politics. Punk, in Mike's view, while still important politically, did not focus the audience squarely on the meaning of the music. Rather, punk music

---

4. The interviewee is referring to the Beatles album *Sgt. Pepper's Lonely Hearts Club Band*, released in June 1967 on the Parlophone label. At the time of its release, the album was considered anthemic of the countercultural movement (see, for example, Martin and Hornsby 1979).

acted as a medium for drawing out emotions and inspiring particular modes of thought among the audience that combined to underpin and nurture a radical sensibility. Mike's description of his post-punk involvement with the free party scene of the mid-1980s is also insightful in terms of mapping the development of his political sensibility through his changing musical taste. Punctuated by natural events such as the summer solstice—the latter being marked by a gathering at Stonehenge in the south of England—the free parties brought aging members of the original 1960s counterculture together with anarcho-punks and "crusties" (also referred to in the U.K. media as New Age Travellers because of their nomadic existence; see McKay 1996; Hetherington 1998; Martin 2002). Although the music featured at free parties was, generally speaking, not political in itself (a regular feature at the Stonehenge festival was 1960s "space rock" band Hawkwind[5]), these events are generally acknowledged as a kernel for a new wave of DIY political groups, such as the Anti-Road Protest, Reclaim the Streets, and The Land is Ours (see McKay 1998). In recounting his biographical journey through what could be termed this alternative political landscape, from punk to the free party scene, Mike showed that his focus had moved beyond the specificities of music to the subversive synergies that he argued emerged from music-infused settings:

> With the free festivals, it's this kind of notion that you've got, on the one hand . . . kind of social occasions, blah, blah, blah, an' then you've got like political action. Ehm, and the two don't normally go together. Y'know, if you go on a sort of march against, eh, I don't know, an anti-apartheid march, then, that's one thing. An' then, y'know, if you go to a party that's another thing. But somehow or another those free festivals put the two together and made it very clear. . . . Not

---

5. Formed in London during the late 1960s, Hawkwind (whose early lineup included bassist Ian "Lemmy" Kilmister, who went on to form heavy metal band Motörhead) was a favorite on the British festival scene of the 1970s. Hawkwind combined elements of acid, progressive, and blues rock with an early use of electronic synthesizers and an emphasis on science-fiction themes in song lyrics, which earned its sound the name "space rock" among music journalists.

just, eh, not just theoretical politics, it's got a sort of reality about it.

Significantly, however, throughout this account of his transitional journey through musical scenes and political discourses, Mike retained a sense of himself as an "old hippie." Notwithstanding the fundamental flaws he identified in the hippie rhetoric, and the hippie scene's misguided understanding of popular music's potential to change the world, Mike continued to place great purchase on the values he had acquired during his hippie youth and the ways in which he felt these had informed his subsequent biographical development. This would suggest that, whatever the term "hippie" expressed in a 1960s context, this proved less important in the long term than the intellectual nourishment that those with a predisposition for radical, counter-hegemonic thought carried forward with them when the problems and contradictions underpinning the hippie concept became evident and they elected to leave the faltering counterculture behind. Thus, Mike observed:

One of the things about being an old hippie . . . I mean . . . yes, I still want to change the world, yes, I'm still heavily involved in the kind of politics to do that, yes, I still have spiritual concerns. Eh, whether it grew out of [the counterculture] I don't know, or whether it just grew out of me, y'know, in the sense that I've always had these interests, I've just pursued these interests, y'know [because] I'm a particular kind of a person rather than because I was of that generation. But I sort of feel very easy with certain people of my generation.

Mike was not alone in expressing such views. Other interviewees who identified themselves as old hippies similarly claimed that, while their interest in the countercultural music of the late 1960s had quickly faded and been replaced by other tastes—which, in addition to punk, hard-core, and other musics with radical associations, included jazz and classical music—they felt that their lives had been indelibly stamped by their involvement with hippie beliefs. This is clearly illustrated in the following extract from an interview with Matt, a community project worker from the southeast of England now in his mid-fifties:

A.B.: Do you still see yourself as part of that sixties generation? Do you feel a bond?

Matt: The values remain . . . the idea that humanity is of importance, the idea that economics don't drive everything. Those sort of core values which I believe were true then are true now.

A.B.: And when you talk to other people from your generation who were active in the scene, is that a shared view?

Matt: Certainly among the people I know and work with, yes.

Matt, like Mike, John, Susan, and others whom I interviewed, locates himself within a milieu of like-minded individuals whose shared generational sensibilities, they believed, had evolved from their collective experience of being associated with the late-1960s counterculture. Irrespective of the problems they associated with hippie values and countercultural ideology, all of these interviewees felt that they had taken fundamental inspiration from those beliefs, which had shaped to varying degrees their subsequent lifestyles and political outlook.

Beyond the Political

In addition to discussing the counterculture's investment in music as a driver for political change, a number of people I interviewed highlighted music's impact on their spiritual values and broader lifestyle sensibilities. The notion of spirituality is another aspect of 1960s hippie rhetoric that, during the ensuing decades, has been much maligned and crudely essentialized in popular representations of the hippie lifestyle. This negative depiction is most frequently seen in fictional representations, such as Gillies MacKinnon's 1998 film *Hideous Kinky*, which portrays hippies' experimentation with Eastern religions and mysticism as inherently naive and disrespectful of the broader cultural contexts in which such religious and philosophical practices are embedded. In an essay on hippie culture written during the late

1960s, Stuart Hall suggested that the hippies' turning to Eastern religions such as Buddhism "represent[ed] a return to contemplation and mystical experience" (1968: 8). Seldom represented, however, is the broader spectrum of activities that such experimentation involved and their lasting influence on a range of contemporary, everyday cultural practices. For example, in the fields of health, healing, diet, and education, many of these practices have continued to grow in popularity among Western societies.

Musically too, the influence of Eastern religion and mysticism on Western audiences is arguably quite poorly represented in existing accounts of the counterculture. Part of the problem with such accounts relates to their overemphasis on amplified rock music which, although it was a mainstay of the late 1960s era, leads to a skewed account of the rich variety of musicians and music that characterized the countercultural era (Allen 2004). Thus, while much attention is paid to artists such as the Beatles, the Rolling Stones, and Jimi Hendrix, little space is given to the contribution of groups such as the Incredible String Band, the Third Ear Band, Quintessence, or the early recordings of Tyrannosaurus Rex[6] to the countercultural soundscape. However, such groups, despite their gentler, more acoustically oriented styles, were as revered in some quarters of the counterculture as their heavier, more rock-oriented counterparts. The music of groups such as the Incredible String Band, rather than mounting sonically and/or lyrically aggressive attacks on the political arena of the late 1960s, traded in altogether more esoteric forms of countercultural politics—centering on abstract prose and experimentation with musical timbres and rhythms drawn from the Middle East and sub-Indian continent. In some cases, this "other face" of countercultural music appears to have had a more lasting impression on aging hippie audiences than did the music of heavier-sounding groups more typically associated with the counterculture. Speaking

---

6. Originally comprising the duo Marc Bolan and Steve Peregrin Took, Tyrannosaurus Rex made early acoustic recordings that many consider to be quintessential examples of countercultural music. Tyrannosaurus Rex reemerged in the early 1970s as the Bolan-led glam rock combo T. Rex.

about his involvement with the counterculture and the role of music within, John, the Englishman in his late fifties, offered the following account:

> I mean, if we have to relate [the counterculture] to music, which, I think, is the significant thing for me anyway, it was the more esoteric music. It was what we would now call World Music, but in those days it was just like "weird" music. And, eh, there was a band which you may remember called the Incredible String Band, who were and still are of supreme importance to me. . . . I consider them one of the forerunners of what we now call World Music because they were playing exotic instruments in those days. They were doing Arabic things and Middle Eastern stuff, Indian and goodness knows what else, before it was, y'know, fashionable.[7]

Much discussion and debate have focused on the concept of "World Music" because of both the highly selective and canonical discourses that surround this title and also the way it lends exoticism to and effectively "Others" a range of apparently diverse and diffuse musics purely on the grounds of their non-Western origins (see Frith 2000). Ironically, at some level, it is precisely the appropriation of non-Western music by Western rock musicians during the late 1960s and beyond that created a demand for, and fetishization of, such music among Western listeners. John was both highly aware of these debates

---

7. The Incredible String Band attracted much attention during its appearance at the original Woodstock festival in August 1969. Although generally cited as a model for contemporary rock festivals and mega-events (see Garofalo 1992; Laing 2004), Woodstock also reflected an increasing openness on the part of white, Western audiences to non-Western musical styles. In addition to the Incredible String Band, the sitar music of Ravi Shankar, the simulated ragga style of Stephen Stills in his acoustic guitar solo on Crosby, Stills and Nash's "Suite: Judy Blue Eyes," and the mixolydian scales of then emergent electric guitar virtuoso Carlos Santana added a distinctly non-Western flavor to the rock and blues–influenced music of other featured artists, such as Jimi Hendrix, Creedence Clearwater Revival, and Canned Heat. In this sense, Woodstock could, at one level, also be regarded as a kernel for the World Music events that were to follow in the future.

and immensely sensitive to the way in which his status as a white, middle-class, middle-aged professional implicated him within them. In an attempt to resolve this issue, John turned to issues of definition and critical canons as these informed countercultural music. For John, the Incredible String Band, and other groups from the era he preferred, registered much less in such canons than groups such as the Beatles and the Rolling Stones, which, in John's opinion, had contributed far more to the fetishization of non-Western musics. As such, claimed John, in listening to World Music today, he is able to appreciate it with a far more "informed" and respectful ear than those who entered this sphere of musical consumption via what he considered to be the more passé experiments of the Beatles and others. For John, the Incredible String Band and similar artists retained a far more spiritual connection with the non-Western music they appropriated than some of their more famous and commercially successful peers. Indeed, it was the notion of spirituality rather than political engagement through which John articulated his ongoing relationship with countercultural values. Asked if he felt the politics of the countercultural generation had influenced his current political outlook, John lamented: "Tony Blair [former British prime minister] was my generation. And I don't feel part of his generation at all." Rather, in John's case, what he appears to have taken forward with him from the countercultural era is spiritual nourishment. Thus, as he explained, again with reference to the Incredible String Band:

> The [Incredible] String Band were, I think I said it earlier, they were much more surreal [and] literate, they would pluck ideas from all sorts of literary sources and spiritual sources. I'm not a religious person, but I consider myself a very spiritual person. And, y'know, that's a different argument, but I consider that music is a very important thing in that respect. And the String Band to me were very important because they actually touched all sorts of bases.

As this account illustrates, in John's biographical development, the musical tastes and influences he acquired as a teenager during the late 1960s were inherently linked.

Dropping Out, Dropping In?

As noted earlier in this chapter, academic accounts of the counter-culture tend to represent it as both a white and a purely middle-class concern (see, for example, Roszak 1969 and Willis 1978). Indeed, a prominent criticism of countercultural politics has focused on the alleged hypocrisy of a white middle-class youth experimenting with alternative lifestyles before conveniently dropping back in to mainstream society and picking up where their lives had left off. Such representations of the counterculture, and its failings, are commonplace. However, as some of those who participated in the research for this book explained, these representations are not always accurate portrayals of the post-countercultural experience. For one thing, it was pointed out that the counterculture, particularly in the United Kingdom, was not as uniformly middle class as popular representations maintain. Indeed, the expansion of higher education during the mid-1960s saw increasing numbers of lower-middle-class and working-class school dropouts going to university, an opportunity that also brought a number of these young people into contact with countercultural groups and beliefs. As several interviewees who had found themselves in this situation explained, although the counterculture initially seemed appealing, experimenting with alternative lifestyles and dropping out of the system presented other problems, particularly for those from working-class backgrounds. Thus, as Mike, the Englishman in his mid-fifties, observed:

> We were all sort of dropping out an', eh, blowing our careers, but once it all sort of flopped, which it did in the end, y'know, the fact was those of us from the working-class backgrounds were left with nothing. Y'know, we didn't have anything then. Y'know, what we had was the possibility of a factory job, again.

In many ways, this account illustrates how the counterculture not only brought youth from different class backgrounds together but also, at some level, reproduced class inequalities as these played out between the parent cultures of the mixed-class hippie youth. Such experience has a close bearing on how some interviewees reflected on and rationalized the impact of the counterculture on their subsequent attitude toward countercultural politics. Among a number of interviewees of working-class origin who had passed through the counterculture on their way to adulthood, their negative experiences as young hippie dropouts had served as a catalyst for a subsequent, ongoing, critical engagement with countercultural politics. As Julie, a woman from the southeast of England in her late fifties, observed: "I don't think anybody really knew what I was doing. My family practically disowned me. But at the same time, I wouldn't say I really clicked with any of the, what you would call, cooler hippies, who seemed somehow made for that existence."

Mike concurred with and elaborated on this view, suggesting that it was only with the benefit of hindsight and the more sustained reflection achieved through adulthood that he had been able to critically deconstruct his countercultural experience and make sense of it on his own terms. Thus, he said: "When I was like nineteen . . . I wasn't very class conscious at all. . . . I only knew that certain people made me feel like, they were puttin' me down. An' it was only later that [I could] really define where I stood."

For the most part, however, those interviewees who expressed a former allegiance to the counterculture, or continued to identify themselves as old hippies, were quite positive about what the late 1960s achieved in terms of creating social change in the world. For many, this contribution could not be attributed to any one element of the era, the counterculture and its music included, but was rather a facet of a large-scale push among many disparate elements of society to bring about social change. In this sense, the sentiments of interviewees echoed Roszak's (1969) argument that the counterculture was actually a populist umbrella term for a variety of interest groups and social causes, of which the "hippie" movement was only a more spectacular and, perhaps, superficial aspect. Julie and Mike both suggested that the significance of the 1960s as a decade of radical social change could only be truly appreciated by comprehending the broader spectrum of issues at stake and how these were addressed. As Mike put it:

I think [the 1960s were] times of great, great change. The world was really changing, and if you look back pre-sixties to what we have now, the sixties defines the difference. . . . Homosexuality was illegal . . . when a woman got pregnant [there were] shotgun weddings, y'know. Eh, the kind of foods we eat, everything. I mean things really shifted. . . . And we were just part of that really. . . . And, yes, it was full of kind of ludicrousness, and pretension and gurus walking about [laughs] and lots of people doing themselves in with drugs. . . . But at the same time there was a real sort of openness, of possibility.

This, above all, was the lasting view that many people I interviewed appeared to subscribe to. They did not claim that music and its associated stylistic and sociopolitical ideologies were in any way centrally responsible for the social and cultural changes that emanated from the 1960s. Rather, they suggested that music, musicians, and music audiences were simply some of the voices among the many that called for, and were ultimately successful in bringing about, a degree of social and cultural reform within the wider social and cultural milieu of the 1960s and early 1970s.

The Punk Perspective

Among older punks too, much of what was related in interviews concerned to a greater or lesser degree the mark left on them by the political legacy of punk. Like the counterculture, punk aligned itself with a range of sociopolitical issues. In the United Kingdom, for example, the formation of the Rock Against Racism (RAR) movement in the late 1970s saw punk and new wave groups such as the Clash, X-Ray Spex, Elvis Costello and the Attractions, and the Tom Robinson Band performing at open-air concerts organized by RAR (Frith and Street 1992). Similarly, in the German city of Hannover, punk took the form of a semi-organized protest—*die Choastage* (Chaos Days)—against what many participants regarded as the rampant capitalism of the Western world (Geiling 1995, 1996), while in the Eastern Bloc, punk became the voice of a disenchanted youth against a backdrop of a failing Communist system (Szemere 1992). From the outset then, punk was rather more than the spectacular, antisocial style often portrayed in the mass media. Wearing its political dissatisfactions on its sleeve, punk frequently engaged with *local* issues—those that affected and/or frustrated its followers on a day-to-day basis (Bennett 2001a).

Although undoubtedly punk began as a youth-based movement, the continuing associations made between youth and punk in the popular media and elsewhere since the 1970s have contributed to a general misperception of punk's ongoing political significance. As with punk style, in popular media representations the political dimensions of punk continue to be mapped as an extension of youth disempowerment, lack of norms, and attendant frustration as these pertained in the late 1970s. Consequently, the historical legacy of punk has been read largely in these terms—that is, as a heat of the moment, youth-led revolt with no long-term impact or influence on those who followed punk and its attendant sociocultural sensibilities. Indeed, the post-punk careers and personal reflections of some of those individuals once stridently associated with the movement have done little to dispel the belief in punk's inherent temporality. For example, one-time punk and *New Musical Express* (*NME*) journalist, Julie Burchill, has since been unequivocally dismissive of punk's alleged anarchism. Claiming that she associated with punk primarily in order to get a journalism job with *NME*, Burchill subsequently was quoted as saying, "Punk was over in two years. That was the only damn good thing about it."[8]

More recently, the dominance of such representations among aging spokespeople of the punk generation has been challenged by alternative takes on the punk legacy, such as that presented in Jim Lindberg's (2007) book *Punk Rock Dad: No Rules, Just Real Life*. Lindberg, front man for California-based punk band Pennywise, portrays in detail his lifestyle as an aging punk and how it must be carefully balanced with married life and bringing up three daughters. On the way, Lindberg relates how his long-term association with punk has influenced various facets of his life and worldview. Similarly, Henry Rollins, former front man for American anarcho-punk band Black Flag (see Gosling 2004), now hosts his own punk-style talk TV show on the Independent Film Channel (a U.S. independent television channel).

---

8. See http://www.thejc.com/articles/julie-burchill-brash-outspoken-and-wishing-she-was-jewish (accessed February 16, 2009).

During the show, Rollins interviews guests such as Iggy Pop and Marilyn Manson, delivers humorous and satirical monologues, and features uncensored musical performances by groups such as the New York Dolls, the Stooges, and Placebo. These examples of aging punks continuing to work with and present punk-influenced discourses to a broader public suggest the possibility of an alternative reading of the punk legacy. Punk remains the basis for a more long-standing worldview among many of those individuals who came of age during the punk era and took inspiration from its message of anarchy and rebellion—however flawed it may have been.

What Price Anarchy?

In his highly accomplished study of punk music and style, *One Chord Wonders*, Laing (1985) observes that in punk terms "anarchy" was never in any sense a formulated political statement but rather a "play" on politics embedded within punk's aural and visual battery of shock tactics. Elaborating on this, Laing notes how, in the song that allegedly defined anarchy as a lynchpin of punk's assault on the sensibilities of mainstream society, the Sex Pistols' "Anarchy in the UK," the word "anarchy" is vocally manipulated by singer Johnny Rotten in such a way that it assumes a largely ironic resonance. Underlying Laing's argument is a view, widely espoused, that many of the punk youth of the late 1970s were excited primarily by the subversive possibilities of "anarchy" rather than by a commitment to its practical realization. Punk youth in the late 1970s idealized the notion of anarchy as a vehicle for social change without ever stopping to contemplate the real-world implications of such ideals or the practical obstacles in the way of their realization.

The expressed attitudes of older punks toward the ideals of their youth were telling. As with the aging hippies referred to earlier in this chapter, when reflecting on their youth, older punks articulated a highly reflexive awareness of the naïveté inherent in their earlier music-inspired political beliefs. At the same time, however, many claimed to have reappraised and reevaluated such beliefs. In doing so, they had not dismissed these beliefs out of hand; rather, they had toned them down and reworked them in ways they believed functioned more credibly as political ideas and attendant lifestyle projects for their adult selves. Thus, in looking back on his youth involvement in punk and comparing it with his present outlook, Ned, a British punk in his mid-forties, observed:

> I think when you're a teenager, it's a bit frustrating because you want to change the whole world and you want to change it right now and you want everything to be good, the way you see good as being. And it makes you angry that you haven't really got any power to do anything about it. And as you get older, you do maintain your idealism, but you get a bit more sensible about what kind of impact you can have yourself, and [realize] that things take a long time to change, and that it's not possible to change everything at once. But, as long as you act right in your life and do the things that you can which will influence the people around you, then you're doing the best that you can, so you're a lot less angry about things.

For many aging punks, the operationalization of this political worldview involved a number of common features. These included support for global causes, such as the anticapitalist movement, and an ardent interest—or often proactive involvement—in single-issue political concerns, such as environmentalism, animal rights, and the Anti-Road Protest. Among those aging punks I interviewed who continued to play in bands, staging and participating in benefit concerts for these and other causes were regularly cited as an important aspect of their gigging calendar.

On other occasions, aging punks stressed the importance of tolerance and respect for others as lessons they had learned from punk. For many, such principles were in themselves a form of political behavior that supplanted their earlier interest in radical politics as a more plausible pathway toward creating a sustainable and equitable society. This viewpoint was effectively summed up by Sally, a punk from South Australia in her late forties:

> I still believe in the same things. I've probably rounded them off more. [I'm not] taking it all in as gospel, so's to speak, as we

did then. Like anarchy and things like that. Obviously, you've gotta live on this planet, and I don't think anarchy as a political [idea] would work . . . but I think some of the things about the anarchy thing [were] good . . . the getting along with people. You see, that was the thing about punk, I think. We looked upon it like there was this bunch of social misfits that got together.

Interestingly, in contrast to the aging hippies, who frequently talked of the absurdity of their countercultural beliefs as teenagers and early twenty-somethings, aging punks, although often self-critical of their earlier punk selves, were at the same time adamant that, from the outset, punk had instilled within them a life-changing experience for the better. Aging punks commonly suggested that punk had played an important part in their transition from youth to adulthood, providing them with a street-wise outlook and a sense of realism. Many intimated that their path to becoming fully rounded, critically aware individuals dated in considerable part from their initial involvement with punk and their internalization of the punk ethic. Moreover, notwithstanding the critical reevaluation of their punk identity over time, many older punks suggested that their basic sense of self continued to be informed by the punk ideology. Indeed, a number of interviewees considered themselves to be the very essence of a "punk personality," as illustrated in the following extract from an interview with Stu, an English punk in his early fifties:

There's still a part of me that embraces the rebelliousness, the sort of, ehm, "stick your two fingers up at the establishment," the sort of political nature of it, the fact that "Yeah, this is what I like, an', therefore, why can't I do it?" . . . [Punk] was a pivotal part of my life that has influenced everything since . . . my musical influences, an' the way I think about things. . . . I can actually chart it back to a certain period where, eh, y'know, things suddenly became different. And because you're different and, y'know, the rest of society sees that difference as bad [it] has an influence. An' you realize, well, "Maybe [pauses] everything's not as bad as it seems, or as people portray it," an' it gives you a sort of outsider feel.

Such an "outsider feel" was related on various occasions by aging punks as they sought to describe how their view of the world was often so diametrically opposed to others that they often found themselves in situations of conflict. Similarly, many interviewees, when asked how they felt their political opinions had been actively shaped by their involvement with punk, spoke openly of an ongoing disdain for what they considered mainstream political views, social norms, and "traditional" cultural values. This position was summed up accurately by Chris, an English punk in his mid-forties, who offered the following observation:

> I can sit here and watch the news, and give it from a punk per-
> spective, I always have done. . . . September the eleventh was
> a classic example. Everybody said, 'Isn't it terrible," an' I said,
> "I'm surprised it didn't happen earlier." An' they're going,
> "Why are you thinking that?" And I was like, "American for-
> eign policy." But people don't know, do they? They look at you
> as if you're mad when you say things like that. Or Lady Diana
> dying. That was another [example]. I just look at most of the
> British society as being quite mad, when they react like that.

Such staunch criticism of mainstream politics and associated sociocultural values permeated all of my interviews with aging punks in the United Kingdom and Australia. Of all the sentiments that seemed to bind aging punks, translocally speaking, into an affective scene, a common rhetoric of alternative ideology based on a rejection of mainstream political parties and, in some cases, the notion of political ideology itself was clearly marked.

Aging punks also offered interesting responses to the question of whether or not they felt that punk had actually transformed society in any meaningful or positive way. A standard populist response to such a question is that punk's opposition to the state and civil society was largely played out at the level of symbolism and ritual, with little in the way of a formulated counter-hegemonic attack on mainstream political values to carry it forward beyond an initial flurry of visual and aural shock tactics. Indeed, according to Hebdige (1988), punk was, in the final analysis, emblematic of a dawning postmodern age. For Hebdige, punk functioned as a spectacular, yet empty, signifier offering no capacity for momentum; according to Hebdige, the passing of punk icon Sid Vicious (who died from a heroin overdose in New York City on February 2, 1979, at the age of twenty-one) also marked the passing of punk itself.

Among many interviewees, however, the notion that punk's critical moment was so temporally positioned was erroneous. Equally, their view that the punk legacy could only be read in terms of a romanticized vision of punk tied to its brief lifespan as a highly mediatized—and primarily British and American—object of a moral panic, was incorrect. Like those interviewees who reflected on the musical longevity of punk (see Chapter 5), in assessing punk's potential to contribute to patterns of social change, aging punks often pointed to the resurgence of punk as a more underground movement during the early 1980s and its global development as a post-youth movement. The more long-term significance of punk as a politicized movement, it was argued, could only be fully appreciated if one stopped thinking of it in terms of a late 1970s Anglo-American youth cultural movement and instead engaged with the translocal connections between multigenerational punk scenes dotted around the globe. Only then, it was argued, could one truly understand and appreciate the role played by punk in major moments of social and economic change during the late twentieth and early twenty-first centuries. As with the aging hippies' views on countercultural music, aging punks stopped short of citing punk music itself as a major catalyst for social change. However, many aging punk interviewees felt that punk had lent its voice and support to a variety of sociopolitical causes in very incisive ways. Chris, for example, supplied his own highly detailed and articulate reading of punk's place in the global array of social movements and causes to have characterized the last three decades:

> Punk attitude, I see it as informing everything from the anti-globalization movement down to, eh, the hunting bans com-

ing in now. . . . All through the eighties there was an 'ell of a lot o' punks out hunt sabbing.[9] Y'know what I mean, stuff like that. . . . Your average British response [is], "Oh, things won't change. Why bother tryin' to change anything?" I've seen things change in the course of twenty-five years. An' a lot o' them battles, y'know, in the fall of Eastern Europe, for instance. [There was a m]assive punk influence in that, and the underground. An, y'know, I didn't think I'd ever see the Berlin Wall come down, y'know what I mean. But, [punk is] worldwide, an' it's . . . involved with every movement of progressive social change there is, I'd say. Whether that's been outside the nuke bases or squattin' [in] an empty building. I see it as all linked, y'know what I mean.

This observation demonstrates something of the breadth of contemporary sociohistorical and cultural transitions with which the aging punks in my interview sample identified. Moreover, such observations and the sentiments they elicited were not restricted to those who identified themselves as aging punks. Among aging individuals I encountered in the free dance party scene too, knowledge of such developments and others—for example, the anticapitalist movement— was frequently discussed. Indeed, a number of those interviewed claimed to have found their way into the free party scene through prior involvement with anarcho-punk movements, both in the United Kingdom and elsewhere. Many had firsthand experience of living in squats, being involved in hunt "sabbing," environmental activism, and other related activities. It was noted previously how one aging hippie described his transition through the hippie scene, the punk scene, and, later, the free party scene, identifying in each a subversive element triggered by an understanding of the musical soundscape as providing space for the nurturing of a critical sensibility. Other

---

9. The term "sabbing" refers to the sabotage of fox hunting, an activity engaged in by activist groups in the United Kingdom prior to the outlawing of fox hunts in England and Wales with the passing of the Hunting Act in 2004. The Scottish Parliament had passed a law banning fox hunting two years earlier. Fox hunting remains legal in Northern Ireland.

interviewees echoed this observation, suggesting that the transition from anarcho-punk to the free party scene seemed for them an entirely "natural" one, with anarcho punk exuding a tribalism that seemed to find its expression in the free party scene's facilitation of a physical space for those affectively bonded through their disillusionment with mainstream party politics and the mainstream's exclusion of vast tracts of the population who felt they inhabited a social wasteland.

In 1994, British television station Channel 4 screened a short documentary about the Exodus Collective. From its origins as part of the free party scene in Britain, Exodus moved into renovated formerly abandoned and condemned farm buildings near the town of Luton in Bedfordshire and was eventually granted tenancy of the buildings (see Bennett 2001a; Maylon 1998). When interviewed for the documentary, one member of the Exodus Collective, a multigenerational group of people, offered the following comments on how and why the Collective was formed:

> [Exodus is] a group of young and old people who are dedicated to doing something for their lives and others. . . . We're people who could have been called lazy. Not optionally lazy, not, you know, not wanting to work. But sort of gradually getting used to the idea that there's not a lot [of work] about, especially if you're in the excluded group; excluded by color, style, attitude, criminal records, a whole heap of reasons why people are excluded. (cited in TV documentary *Exodus*, broadcast as part of the Channel 4 *Tribe Time TV* series in November 1994; see also Bennett 2001a: 131)

Similar views were expressed among members of another U.K.-based dance music collective whom I interviewed in the course of my research. Although not based in shared, communal living, as was the Exodus Collective, members of the group emphasized the strong bonds between them, which emerged through a mutual feeling of being on the margins of society. This is clearly illustrated in the following extract from an interview with Jake, a forty-two-year-old tradesperson from southeast England with a background in and continued links to the free party scene.

A.B.: How did you come to be a part of the free party scene?

Jake: Well, it was through the tribe really.

A.B.: What do you mean by that?

Jake: Well, I was a punk, an' that got me involved in a squat scene. Then slowly building that up, y'know.

A.B.: Building what up?

Jake: Well, I didn't have a job, couldn't afford rent. The squat was a bunch of people like that. We found each other, then we found others through the free party stuff. Things got a bit easier, y'know. I've got a job now, an' a place to live, an' a kid. But, you never lose that sense of having been through that. Still feel like you're on the edge, y'know. These people are my family, really, 'cause they've all been through it. We relate to each other. We help each other out.

When viewed in this context, the legacy of punk—its impact on the political values and worldview of those associated it—can be read in terms of a long-term and ongoing engagement with the socioeconomic fallout of a postindustrial society that increasingly functions to exclude groups and individuals. As noted earlier in the chapter, for many aging punks this manifests itself through an ongoing, ardent association with punk values—albeit often in toned-down ways that are considered to cohere with an aging punk lifestyle. For others, punk sensibilities of difference and marginalization have been rearticulated through the free party scene, which, as was illustrated in Chapter 5, has also become increasingly multigenerational. It offers spaces for what Ned, an English punk in his late forties, described as "a more relaxed, chilled out kind of rebellion than the sort that needs to be in your face the whole time." Like the aging members of the straight edge scene investigated by Haenfler (2006), although older members of the free party scene have toned down their anti-hegemonic practices and sensibilities, middle-aged members of the dance party scene and their younger counterparts continue to have much in common. In the case of the free party scene, this includes an emphasis on nonviolence, nonsexist and nonracist behavior, and moderate drug and alcohol consumption. Additionally, although now employed in a variety of occupations, members of the party scene generally have relatively modest lifestyles. To a great extent, all of these characteristics appear to chime with a felt need to find an alternative style of living as a means of negotiating what are considered to be the excesses and other pathological tendencies of postindustrial, neoliberal consumer capitalism.

As this chapter has illustrated, aging popular music audiences identify highly varied connections between their ongoing musical influences and their political outlook on the world. Throughout their adult lives, aging music fans associated with various scenes—examples in this chapter have included hippie, punk, and the free party movement—have deeply reflected on the relationship between music and politics and the ways in which this relationship impacts on them as individuals. As the various accounts cited in this chapter indicate, for many of those who have been deeply involved in music-driven scenes with a political dimension, their post-youth lives have included an extensive reassessment of the significance of such musico-cultural experiences. Within this, the relative merits—and shortcomings—of music as a means through which to engage with politics have been continually reassessed. While by no means universally dismissive of music's role in fostering political values, many aging fans now appear to view music more as a catalyst for forms of political engagement than as a fundamental element in their developing political sensibilities and a political outlook on the world. The aging process, it appears, has fostered new, more critically informed opinions on the capacity of music to engineer social change in the more dramatic, large-scale ways in which this was often envisaged by interviewees during their youth. At the same time, however, many aging fans are candid about the legacy of scenes such as the counterculture and punk, pointing to their role in effecting more subtle changes in the social fabric and opening up spaces for the articulation of alternative political, cultural, and spiritual values.

Conclusion

Too Old to Rock and Roll?

We joke about listening to the Ramones in the old people's home,
at eighty or whatever. 'Cause you can't imagine not enjoying
it anymore when you get to a certain age. And when you see,
y'know, . . . rock stars like Mick Jagger and Bob Dylan, they're
sixty-two and they're still on the road and everything. It does give
you hope that people's music obsessions stay with them for their
whole lives and you don't have to give up on it and start playing
lawn bowls. (Suzy, Australian punk, aged forty-eight)

In the introduction to this book, it was noted that, although the
aging popular music fan is by no means a unique product of late
modernity, the relationship between popular music, media, and
consumption that emerged during the 1950s did have a significant
bearing on the everyday importance of popular music from there on
as a cultural form and a cultural resource. From this point in history
onward, questions of musical ownership became increasingly complex, as global icons, genres, texts, and associated consumer items,
such as fashion and literature, forged new understandings of identity,
lifestyle, and cultural belonging as these were understood and articulated by successive youth audiences. The key question underpinning
the book has been whether, and how, such influences have remained
with postwar generations in their post-youth lives. The average age
of the people interviewed for this book was between forty-five and
fifty-five. At the close of each interview, the interviewee was invited
to reflect on how he or she might respond to and make use of popular music in everyday life beyond his or her seventieth birthday. The
above observation from Suzy is broadly representative of the response
most interviewees came up with when asked this question. There

was a widespread belief among interviewees that their popular music tastes and associated cultural practices had had such a fundamental effect on their lives to date that envisaging a time without music was unimaginable. Remarks such as "listening to Jimi Hendrix in the nursing home" and "going clubbing with my Zimmer frame [walker]" were common.

Offered in a lighthearted fashion as such comments often were, they nevertheless point to a time in the near future when the majority of third age citizens will be members of the baby-boomer and post-boomer generations. The implications of this reality for leisure and lifestyle provision among the aged are clear. A critical point indicated throughout this book is that leisure and lifestyle preferences once firmly associated with youth are increasingly a multigenerational feature of late modern societies and will soon extend well into the third age. Some evidence of this shift can already be seen. For example, during the fieldwork conducted in France for this book, Pierre, a Frenchman in his mid-fifties, informed me that the "tea dances" he helped organize for pensioners now featured Beatles music alongside standards from the forties and fifties. This, he said, had been done after the patrons themselves had requested more "modern" music to dance to.

The importance of popular music as an aspect of individual identity and its interweaving with choices about lifestyle, consumption, and the significance of material culture in contemporary everyday life were very much in the minds of interviewees when they reflected on their transition to later life. Such was the centrality of music, and the necessity of having it around them, that many interviewees said they could simply not imagine a time when they would be happy to give this up and move into a nursing home or other type of shared accommodation where access to music, and associated personal effects, might be more limited. Within this sentiment, the necessity of having the freedom to construct an individual soundscape of favorite music was viewed in equal importance to being surrounded by CDs, DVDs, and good-quality sound reproduction equipment. When asked about the possible benefits of iPod technology in this respect, responses were quite mixed. Some agreed that this technology would definitely be an advantage, not least in that, in addition to facilitating private listening, it allowed for the highly compact storing of vast amounts of music. Others, however, took a more ambivalent stance. Thus, as Stu, an English punk in his mid-forties, observed: "I don't like listening to music through small headphone speakers. It's not the same." Another interviewee, Paul, an fifty-year-old Englishman, exclaimed: "Well, iPods, hmm, you can have what, a million songs on there [laughs]? But it's not the same as having a whacking great shelf of vinyl, CDs, and DVDs, is it?"

Among the musicians in my interview sample, a greater confidence, not to say comfort, was to be found in technology, especially home-recording technology and its associated benefits in facilitating an ongoing music-making interest in old age. Predicting a time when age might limit mobility and also bring with it failing health, access to high-quality, easy-to-operate digital recording equipment was considered key to remaining active and creative as a music-maker in later life. As John, a guitarist in his late forties, commented: "I can't imagine playing in bands all my life, going to gigs, setting up and tearing down stuff. It's hard work. But I can imagine recording stuff at home. The gear is so light and portable now. It doesn't matter where you are. All you need is a laptop, guitar, and drum machine. Y'know, too easy."

Commenting on societal expectations of the elderly, interviewees provided accounts that were also suggestive of significant changes ahead in terms of how baby-boomer and post-boomer individuals may construct their identities as third age citizens. Many expressed concern about how current stereotypes regarding expectations and aspirations among third age populations might impact on their desire for individualism and freedom in relation to issues of identity and lifestyle. Others lamented the way in which aging was seen to bring with it a societal expectation that one would adopt a more conservative outlook on life and a concomitant abandonment of the ideals associated with one's younger years. In an often highly vocal opposition to this notion, many interviewees foresaw themselves as third age citizens who would remain acutely opinionated and politically motivated. Thus, as Andrew, an Australian punk in his late forties, observed:

> People say with aging that you get conservative. People have said that to me since I was about fifteen I suppose. Y'know,

"Oh, you're idealistic, you're young, you'll learn otherwise." Well, I'm forty-eight now and I haven't learned anything apart from becoming more deeply committed to the sort of ideas I had then and knowing more about it. And, you occasionally hear and see people interviewed in their seventies and eighties that haven't lost it. . . . So I don't see any reason apart from fear and egotism perhaps that would force people into becoming more conservative. I doubt I'll be more conservative. I imagine I'll get more radical and sort of react against the kids that do seem a bit conservative.

At the same time, however, physical aging was associated with some limitations, particularly in relation to the importance many attributed to musical involvement as an embodied experience. Many interviewees felt that age should be no object in relation to clubbing, going to gigs, and so on; however, they expressed concern about the reality of this desire in a sphere of popular culture and leisure that has yet to embrace in a practical sense the participation of elderly individuals in such activities. While there was much lighthearted discussion about being the "oldest clubber in town,"[1] at the same time interviewees were very aware that clubs and venues may, by the nature of their physical dimensions, impose obstacles for elderly people. This, in turn, led to talk about the possible need for special facilities: "How about an OAP[2] chill-out room!" suggested Jill, an aging English clubber, only half-jokingly.

Another concern among interviewees was that the possible onset of physical and/or mental infirmity in later life might result in a dependence on others. For many, this scenario posed a threat to the preservation of a lifestyle based on alternative values gleaned from a

---

1. The interviewee is parodying here the novelty song "The Oldest Swinger in Town," written and recorded by British club entertainer Fred Wedlock in the early 1980s.

2. OAP is an abbreviation for "old age pensioner," a term applied to women (aged sixty plus) and men (aged sixty-five plus) in the United Kingdom who are eligible for retirement, state pension, associated state benefits, and subsidies—for example, for bus and rail travel.

lifetime's investment in popular musics, such as punk or dance, and the aesthetic and political sensibilities associated with these. Not surprisingly, many interviewees protested that to be denied access to practices and resources associated with such lifestyles would negatively affect their identity and thus compromise their sense of cultural and political citizenship.

Again, this issue has important ramifications for the provision of leisure and recreation among the aging. Currently, such provision is based largely on organized, institutionalized sites and events. Among those interviewed for this book, there was great hope that the individual, everyday forms of leisure and activities they had constructed around their musical tastes could be continued into later life. As Jed, an aging punk in his mid-forties, exclaimed: "My life has been about DIY. I can't imagine myself sitting in a wheelchair having everything done for me. That's not me, y'know."

Research on cultural issues relating to aging and lifestyle is still at an early stage of development. With the exception of a few studies, notably Blaikie's *Ageing and Popular Culture* (1999) (see also Harrington and Bielby 1995; Gauntlett and Hill 1999; Hunt 2005), the literature on aging is still predominantly concerned with clinical and health-related issues and a concomitant focus on care and medical support for the elderly (see, for example, Ames et al., 2007; Gray et al., 2007; Moore and Haralambous 2007). As each of the anecdotal accounts offered previously indicates, future care and intervention policy on the part of welfare and health services working with third age citizens will demand greater emphasis on catering to the individual, everyday leisure practices of such individuals, and the facilitation of spaces that accommodate such needs.

For those individuals referred to in this chapter, as well as others whose observations are included throughout this book, it is patently clear that the individual identities and lifestyles they have created for themselves through the cultural lens of popular music bespeak a heightened reflexivity and agency that are characteristic aspects of late modernity. A critical feature of the heightened reflexivity of late modern individuals is their use of media and cultural resources in fostering individual and collective projects of identity and lifestyle. One of the key arguments presented in this book is that such identity and lifestyle projects remain with individuals as they traverse the life course. The first generation of individuals to be born into a fully mediatized, fully consumerized Western world is now approaching later life. These individuals carry with them the expectation of retaining control over their lifestyle preferences and practices as they enter the third age. As this book has endeavored to illustrate, popular music and its associated cultural practices continue to play a key role in the lives of many aging individuals, and this appears set to remain the case as such individuals make the transition to later life.

Appendix

A Note on Methodology

Each of the four case studies presented in Part II of the book draws on original ethnographic research conducted over a five-year period between 2002 and 2007. The subjects were aging music fans between the ages of thirty-five and sixty-one. The principal method of collecting data was semistructured, one-on-one interviews (although in two cases participants were interviewed in pairs); there was also a small element of nonparticipant observation in pubs and music venues where clusters of aging music fans gathered (see Chapters 4 and 5). The primary sites for the interviews were East Kent in the United Kingdom, Adelaide in South Australia, and Lille in northern France. Because the project received no direct sources of external funding, fieldwork sites were chosen where access could be guaranteed with the limited financial resources available. The city of Canterbury, in East Kent, was my home for a number of years while I lived in the United Kingdom. Field contacts were initially established through a separate piece of commissioned research I participated in for Surrey Social and Market Research (based at the University of Surrey), focusing on folk and roots music in southeast England. Fieldwork in Adelaide and Lille was enabled through two short-term visiting fellowships I received during the course of the research at the

University of South Australia and the University of Lille in 2005 and 2007, respectively. Key fieldwork contacts in Adelaide were generated largely through word of mouth, with some additional publicizing of the research through a public seminar I presented at the University of South Australia during the early stages of my fellowship visit. In Lille, key fieldwork contacts were secured with the assistance of Dr. Hervé Glevarec (then based at the University of Lille).

In all of the research sites, key fieldwork contacts were used to verbally publicize the research among their personal and professional networks. A snowball sampling method was then applied in generating additional participants for the study. A total of forty-six participants (thirty-seven men and nine women) took part in the research.

In the United Kingdom and Australia, I conducted all of the interviews by myself. In France, the interviews were conducted with the assistance of Dr. Glevarec, who also acted as a translator. In general, interviews lasted between sixty and ninety minutes, and all interviews were recorded on a small, portable voice recorder with the consent of the interviewees. I subsequently transcribed all of the English-language interviews, and Dr. Glevarec consulted with me to provide partial transcriptions and translations of French interviews.

The decision to use one-on-one, semistructured interviews as a data-capture tool was informed by the nature of the research. Most research participants preferred to be interviewed either in their home or in a neutral setting, such as a bar or café, where they could talk in a relaxed and relatively informal way about their individual experiences of being an aging music fan. Some aging fans who continued to actively participate in music scenes occasionally invited me to attend a local gig with them, thus providing some additional level of contextual detail for the research. In South Australia, four participants invited me to visit them at a local community radio station where they worked as voluntary part-time presenters. Again, this opportunity allowed me to experience a physical, everyday context within which aging identities were articulated through and in relation to music-related activities.

The application of categorical descriptors such as (aging) punk, hippie, or clubber/dance music fan to interviewees was based principally upon the interviewees' own description of themselves. Aware of the fact that a number of aging music fans may no longer feel comfortable being associated with such terms, I took care at the start of each interview to clarify with interviewees where they positioned themselves as aging fans. In those cases in which interviewees expressed a sense of dissatisfaction with, or distance from, a particular descriptive term such as "punk" or "hippie," no attempt has been made to associate them with that term in the writing. Similarly, unless interviewees consented to the use of their real names, pseudonyms have been used throughout the book to protect the identities of those who took part in the research.

Bibliography

Allen, D. (2004). A Public Transition: Acoustic and Electric Performances at the Woodstock Festival. In A. Bennett (ed.), *Remembering Woodstock* (pp. 111–126). Aldershot, UK: Ashgate.

Ames, D., Brodaty, H., Chiu, E., Katona, C., Livingstone, G., and Sadavoy, J. (2007). A consensus on defining and measuring treatment benefits in dementia. *International Psychogeriatrics*, 19: 343–344.

Anderson, B. (1983). *Imagined Communities: Reflections on the Origins and Spread of Nationalism*. London: Verso.

Andes, L. (1998). Growing Up Punk: Meaning and Commitment Careers in a Contemporary Youth Subculture. In J. S. Epstein (ed.), *Youth Culture: Identity in a Postmodern World* (pp. 212–231). Oxford, UK: Blackwell.

Ang, I. (1996). *Living Room Wars: Rethinking Audiences for a Postmodern World*. London: Routledge.

Appadurai, A. (1990). Disjuncture and Difference in the Global Cultural Economy. In M. Featherstone (ed.), *Global Culture: Nationalism, Globalisation and Modernity* (pp. 295–310). London: Sage.

Aufheben. (1998). The Politics of Anti-Road Struggle and the Struggles of Anti-Road Politics: The Case of the No. M11 Link Road Campaign. In G. McKay (ed.), *DiY Culture: Party and Protest in Nineties Britain* (pp. 100–128). London: Verso.

Aust, S. (2008). *Der Baader-Meinhof-Komplex* [*The Baader-Meinhof complex*]. Hamburg: Hoffmann und Campe.

Bakhtin, M. M. (1984). *Rabelais and His World*. (H. Isowolsky, trans.). Bloomington, IN: Indiana University Press.

Bannister, M. (2006). *White Boys, White Noise: Masculinities and 1980s Indie Guitar Rock*. Aldershot, UK: Ashgate.

Barnard, M. (1996). *Fashion as Communication*. London: Routledge.

Barthes, R. (1990). The Grain of the Voice. In S. Frith and A. Goodwin (eds.), *On Record: Rock, Pop and the Written Word* (pp. 293–300). London: Routledge.

Bassett, C. (1997). Virtually Gendered: Life in an On-line World. In K. Gelder and S. Thornton (eds.), *The Subcultures Reader* (pp. 537–551). London: Routledge.

Bayton, M. (1990). How Women Become Rock Musicians. In S. Frith and A. Goodwin (eds.), *On Record: Rock, Pop and the Written Word* (pp. 238–257). London: Routledge.

Beck, U. (1992). *The Risk Society: Towards a New Modernity*. (M. Ritter, trans.). London: Sage.

Bell, D. (ed.). (1999). *Woodstock: An Inside Look at the Movie That Shook Up the World and Defined a Generation*. Studio City, CA: Michael Wiese Productions.

Bennett, A. (1997). Going down the pub: The pub rock scene as a resource for the consumption of popular music. *Popular Music*, 16(1): 97–108.

———. (1999). Subcultures or neo-tribes? Rethinking the relationship between youth, style and musical taste. *Sociology*, 33 (3): 599–617.

———. (2000). *Popular Music and Youth Culture: Music, Identity and Place*. London: Macmillan.

———. (2001a). *Cultures of Popular Music*. Buckingham, UK: Open University Press.

———. (2001b). Plug In and Play! UK Indie Guitar Culture. In A. Bennett and K. Dawe (eds.), *Guitar Cultures* (pp. 45–62). Oxford, UK: Berg.

———. (2002). Music, media and urban mythscapes: A study of the Canterbury sound. *Media, Culture and Society*, 24(1): 107–120.

———. (2004a). "Everybody's Happy, Everybody's Free": Representation and Nostalgia in the *Woodstock* Film. In A. Bennett (ed.), *Remembering Woodstock* (pp. 43–54). Aldershot, UK: Ashgate.

———. (2004b). New Tales from Canterbury: The Making of a Virtual Music Scene. In A. Bennett, and R. A. Peterson (eds.), *Music Scenes: Local, Translocal, and Virtual* (pp. 205–20). Nashville, TN: Vanderbilt University Press.

———. (2005). *Culture and Everyday Life*. London: Sage.

———. (2006a). Even Better Than the Real Thing? Understanding the Tribute Band Phenomenon. In S. Homan (ed.), *Access All Eras: Tribute Bands and Global Pop Culture* (pp. 19–31). Buckingham, UK: Open University Press.

———. (2006b). Punk's not dead: The significance of punk rock for an older generation of fans. *Sociology*, 40(1): 219–235.

———. (2007). The forgotten decade: Rethinking the popular music of the 1970s. *Popular Music History*, 2(1): 5–24.

———. (2008a). "Things they do look awful cool": Ageing rock icons and contemporary youth audiences. *Leisure/Loisir*, 32(1): 259–278.

———. (2008b). Towards a cultural sociology of popular music. *Journal of Sociology*, 4(4): 419–432.

———. (2009). "Heritage rock": Rock music, re-presentation and heritage discourse. *Poetics*, 37(5–6): 474–489.

Bennett, A., and Baker, S. (2010). Classic Albums: The Re-presentation of the Rock Album on British Television. In I. Inglis (ed.), *Popular Music on British Television* (pp. 41–54). Aldershot, UK: Ashgate.

Bennett, A., and Kahn-Harris, K. (eds.). (2004). *After Subculture: Critical Studies in Contemporary Youth Culture*. London, Palgrave.

Bennett, A., and Peterson, R. A. (eds.) (2004). *Music Scenes: Local, Translocal, and Virtual*. Nashville, TN: Vanderbilt University Press.

Billig, M. (2000). *Rock 'n' Roll Jews*. Nottingham, UK: Five Leaves.

Blaikie, A. (1999). *Ageing and Popular Culture*. Cambridge, UK: Cambridge University Press.

Blake, M. (2008). Straight shooter. *Mojo*, 179: 95.

Bloustien, G. (2004a). Buffy Night at the Seven Stars: A "Subcultural" Happening at the "Glocal" Level. In A. Bennett and K. Kahn-Harris (eds.), *After Subculture: Critical Studies in Contemporary Youth Culture* (pp. 148–161). London, Palgrave.

———. (2004b). Still Picking Children from the Trees? Re-imagining Woodstock in 21st Century Australia. In A. Bennett (ed.), *Remembering Woodstock* (pp. 127–143). Aldershot, UK: Ashgate.

Breen, M. (1991). A stairway to heaven or a highway to hell? Heavy metal rock music in the 1990s. *Cultural Studies*, 5(2): 191–203.

Breward, C. (1995). *The Culture of Fashion: A New History of Fashionable Dress*. Manchester, UK: Manchester University Press.

Bull, M. (2000). *Sounding Out the City: Personal Stereos and the Management of Everyday Life*. Oxford, UK: Berg.

———. (2005). No dead air! The iPod and the culture of mobile listening. *Leisure Studies*, 24(4): 343–355.

Calcutt, A. (1998). *Arrested Development: Pop Culture and the Erosion of Adulthood*. London: Continuum.

Carrington, B., and Wilson, B. (2002). Global Clubcultures: Cultural Flows and Late Modern Dance Music Culture. In M. Cieslik and G. Pollock (eds.), *Young People in Risk Society: The Restructuring of Youth Identities and Transitions in Late Modernity* (pp. 74–99). Aldershot, UK: Ashgate.

Cavicchi, D. (1998). *Tramps Like Us: Music and Meaning among Springsteen Fans*. New York: Oxford University Press.

Chambers, I. (1976). A Strategy for Living: Black Music and White Subcultures. In S. Hall and T. Jefferson (eds.), *Resistance through Rituals: Youth Subcultures in Post-War Britain* (pp. 157–166). London: Hutchinson.

———. (1985). *Urban Rhythms: Pop Music and Popular Culture*. London: Macmillan.

Chaney, D. (1993). *Fictions of Collective Life: Public Drama in Late Modern Culture*. London: Routledge.

———. (1994). *The Cultural Turn: Scene Setting Essays on Contemporary Cultural History*. London: Routledge.

———. (1996). *Lifestyles*. London: Routledge.

———. (1997). Authenticity and Suburbia. In S. Westwood and J. Williams (eds.), *Imagining Cities: Scripts, Signs and Memories* (pp. 137–148). London: Routledge.

———. (2002). *Cultural Change and Everyday Life*. Basingstoke, UK: Palgrave.

———. (2004). Fragmented Culture and Subcultures. In A. Bennett and K. Kahn-Harris (eds.), *After Subculture: Critical Studies in Contemporary Youth Culture* (pp. 36–48). Basingstoke, UK: Palgrave.

Chatterton, P., and Hollands, R. (2003). *Urban Nightscapes: Youth Cultures, Pleasure Spaces and Corporate Power*. London: Routledge.

Clarke, G. (1990). Defending Ski-Jumpers: A Critique of Theories of Youth Subcultures. In S. Frith and A. Goodwin (eds.), (1990). *On Record: Rock, Pop and the Written Word* (pp. 81–96). London: Routledge.

Clarke, J., Hall, S., Jefferson, T., and Roberts, B. (1976). Subcultures, Cultures and Class: A Theoretical Overview. In S. Hall and T. Jefferson (eds.), *Resistance through Rituals: Youth Subcultures in Post-War Britain* (pp. 9–74). London: Hutchinson.

Clecak, P. (1983). *America's Quest for the Ideal Self: Dissent and Fulfilment in the 60s and 70s*. Oxford, UK: Oxford University Press.

Cohen, Sara (1991). *Rock Culture in Liverpool: Popular Music in the Making*. Oxford, UK: Clarendon Press.

Cohen, Stanley (1987). *Folk Devils and Moral Panics: The Creation of the Mods and Rockers* (3rd ed.). Oxford, UK: Basil Blackwell.

Cooper, L., and Thomas, H. (2002). Growing old gracefully: Social dance in the third age. *Ageing and Society*, 22(6): 689–708.

Cunningham-Burley, S., and Backett-Milburn, K. (1998). The Body, Health and Self in the Middle Years. In S. Nettleton and J. Watson (eds.), *The Body in Everyday Life* (pp. 142–159). London: Routledge.

Denisoff, R. S., and Peterson, R. A. (eds.). (1972). *The Sounds of Social Change*. Chicago: Rand McNally.

Denisoff, R. S., and Romanowski, W. D. (1991). *Risky Business: Rock in Film*. New Brunswick, NJ: Transaction Books.

DeNora, T. (2000). *Music in Everyday Life*. Cambridge, UK: Cambridge University Press.

———. (2004). Music Meaning and Everyday Life. In N. Hnrahan and M. Jacobs (eds), *Blackwell Companion to the Sociology of Culture*. Oxford: Blackwell.

Dowd, T. J., Liddle, K., and Nelson, J. (2004). Music Festivals as Scenes: Examples from Serious Music, Womyn's Music and SkatePunk. In A. Bennett and R. A. Peterson (eds.), *Music Scenes: Local, Translocal, and Virtual* (pp. 149–167). Nashville, TN: Vanderbilt University Press.

Du Bois-Reymond, M. (1998). "I don't want to commit myself yet": Young people's life concepts. *Journal of Youth Studies*, 1(1): 63–79.

Easton, P. (1989). The Rock Music Community. In J. Riordan (ed.), *Soviet Youth Culture*. Bloomington, IN: Indiana University Press.

Ellen, M. (1996). 1996 Hyde Park concert review. *Mojo*, August: 110–111.

Entwistle, J. (2000). *The Fashioned Body: Fashion, Dress and Modern Social Theory*. Cambridge, UK: Polity Press.

Facer, K., and Furlong, R. (2001). Beyond the myth of the "cyberkid": Young people at the margins of the information revolution. *Journal of Youth Studies*, 4(4): 451–469.

Featherstone, M., and Hepworth, M. (1991). The Mask of Ageing and the Postmodern Life Course. In M. Featherstone, M. Hepworth, and B. S. Turner (eds.), *The Body: Social Process and Cultural Theory* (pp. 170–196). London: Sage.

———. (1995). Images of Positive Aging: A Case Study of *Retirement Choice* Magazine. In M. Featherstone and A. Wernick (eds.), *Images of Aging: Cultural Representations of Later Life* (pp. 29–48). London: Routledge.

Finkelstein, J. (1996). *After a Fashion*. Melbourne: Melbourne University Press.

Finnegan, R. (1989). *The Hidden Musicians: Music-Making in an English Town*. Cambridge, UK: Cambridge University Press.

Fiske, J. (1989). *Understanding Popular Culture*. London: Routledge.

Fonarow, W. (1997). The Spatial Organization of the Indie-Guitar Music Gig. In K. Gelder and S. Thornton (eds.), *The Subcultures Reader* (pp. 360–369). London: Routledge.

Fornäs, J., Lindberg, U., and Sernhade, O. (1995). *In Garageland: Rock, Youth and Modernity*. London: Routledge.

Forrest, E. (1994). Generation X. *The Sunday Times* (London). July 10, p. 17.

Frisby, D., and Featherstone, M. (1997). *Simmel on Culture: Selected Writings*. London: Sage.

Frith, S. (1981). The magic that can set you free: The ideology of folk and the myth of rock. *Popular Music*, 1: 159–168.

———. (1983). *Sound Effects: Youth, Leisure and the Politics of Rock*. London: Constable.

———. (1987). Towards an Aesthetic of Popular Music. In R. Leppert and S. McClary (eds.), *Music and Society: The Politics of Composition, Performance and Reception* (pp. 133–151). Cambridge, UK: Cambridge University Press.

———. (1990). Video Pop: Picking Up the Pieces. In S. Frith (ed.), *Facing the Music: Essays on Pop, Rock and Culture* (pp. 88–130). London: Mandarin Books.

———. (2000). The Discourse of World Music. In G. Born and D. Hesmondhalgh (eds.), *Western Music and Its Others: Difference, Representation and Appropriation in Music* (pp. 305–22). Berkeley: University of California Press.

Frith, S., and Horne, H. (1987). *Art into Pop*. London: Methuen.

Frith, S., and McRobbie, A. (1990). Rock and Sexuality. In S. Frith and A. Goodwin (eds.), *On Record: Rock, Pop and the Written Word* (pp. 371–89). London: Routledge.

Frith, S., and Street, J. (1992). Rock against Racism and Red Wedge: From Music to Politics, from Politics to Music. In R. Garofalo (ed.), *Rockin' the Boat: Mass Music and Mass Movements* (pp. 67–80). Boston: South End Press.

Furedi, F. (1997). *The Culture of Fear: Risk-Taking and the Morality of Low Expectation*. London: Cassell.

Garofalo, R. (ed.). (1992). *Rockin' the Boat: Mass Music and Mass Movements*. Boston: South End Press.

Gauntlett, D., and Hill, A. (1999). *TV Living: Television Culture and Everyday Life*. London: Routledge/British Film Institute.

Geertz, C. (1973). *The Interpretation of Cultures*. London: Hutchinson.

Geiling, H. (1995). "Chaos-Tage" in Hannover: Vom Ereignis zum Mythos. *Vorgänge: Zeitschrift für Bürgerrechte und Gesellschaftspolitik*, 4: 1–6.

Geiling, H. (1996). *Das andere Hannover: Jugendkultur zwischen Rebellion und Integration in der Großstadt, Hannover*. Hannover: Offizin Verlag.

Giddens, A. (1991). *Modernity and Self Identity: Self and Society in the Late Modern Age*. Cambridge, UK: Polity Press.

Gill, A. (1998). Deconstruction Fashion: The Making of Unfinished, Decomposing and Re-assembled Clothes. *Fashion Theory*, 2(1): 25–50.

Gilroy, P. (1993). *The Black Atlantic: Modernity and Double Consciou.ness*. London: Verso.

Glevarec, H., and Pinet, M. (2008). From liberalization to fragmentation: A sociology of French radio audiences since the 1990s and the consequences for cultural industries theory. *Media, Culture & Society*, 30(2): 215–238.

Goldman, R. (1992). *Reading Ads Socially*. London: Routledge.

Gosling, T. (2004). "Not for Sale": The Underground Network of Anarcho-Punk. In A. Bennett and R. A. Peterson (eds.), *Music Scenes: Local, Translocal, and Virtual* (pp. 1–15). Nashville, TN: Vanderbilt University Press.

Gray, L., Black, K., Smith, R., and Dorevitch, M. (2007). The supply of inpatient geriatric medical services in Australia. *Internal Medicine Journal*, 37: 370–373.

Gregory, J. (2009). Too young to drink, too old to dance: The influences of age and gender on (non) rave participation. *Dancecult: Journal of Electronic Dance Music Culture*, 1(1): 65–80.

Grossberg, L. (1984). Another boring day in paradise: Rock and roll and the empowerment of everyday life. *Popular Music*, 4: 225–248.

———. (1986). Is there rock after punk? *Critical Studies in Mass Communication*, 3(1): 50–74.

———. (1992). Rock and Roll in Search of an Audience. In J. Lull (ed.), *Popular Music and Communication* (2nd ed.) (pp. 175–197). Newbury Park, CA: Sage.

———. (1994). Is Anybody Listening? Does Anybody Care? On Talking about "The State of Rock." In A. Ross and T. Rose (eds.), *Microphone Fiends: Youth Music and Youth Culture* (pp. 41–58). London: Routledge.

Haenfler, R. (2006). *Straight Edge: Clean-Living Youth, Hardcore Punk, and Social Change.* Piscataway, NJ: Rutgers University Press.

Hall, S. (1968). *The Hippies: An American "Moment."* Birmingham, UK: Centre for Contemporary Cultural Studies, University of Birmingham.

Hall, S., and Jefferson, T. (eds.). (1976). *Resistance through Rituals: Youth Subcultures in Post-War Britain.* London: Hutchinson.

Harrington, C. L., and Bielby, D. (1995). *Soap Fans: Pursuing Pleasure and Making Meaning in Everyday Life.* Philadelphia: Temple University Press.

Harron, M. (1990). McRock: Pop as a Commodity. In S. Frith (ed.), *Facing the Music: Essays on Pop, Rock and Culture* (2nd ed.) (pp. 173–220). London: Mandarin.

Hayes, D. (2006). "Take those old records off the shelf": Youth and music consumption in the postmodern age. *Popular Music and Society*, 29(1): 51–68.

Hebdige, D. (1979). *Subculture: The Meaning of Style.* London: Routledge.

Hebdige, D. (1987). *Cut 'n' Mix: Culture, Identity and Caribbean Music.* London: Routledge.

———. (1988). *Hiding in the Light: On Images and Things.* London: Routledge.

Hetherington, K. (1998). Vanloads of Uproarious Humanity: New Age Travellers and the Utopics of the Countryside. In T. Skelton and G. Valentine (eds.), *Cool Places: Geographies of Youth Culture* (pp. 175–192). London: Routledge.

Hinton, B. (1995). *Message to Love: The Isle of Wight Festivals 1968–70.* Chessington, UK: Castle Communications.

Hodgkinson, J. A. (2004a). The Fanzine Discourse over "Post Rock." In A. Bennett and R. A. Peterson (eds.), *Music Scenes: Local, Translocal, and Virtual* (pp. 221–253). Nashville, TN: Vanderbilt University Press.

Hodkinson, P. (2004). Trans-Local Connections in the Goth Scene. In A. Bennett and R. A. Peterson (eds.), *Music Scenes: Local, Translocal, and Virtual* (pp. 131–149). Nashville, TN: Vanderbilt University Press.

Holland, S. (2004). *Alternative Femininities: Body, Age and Identity.* Oxford, UK: Berg.

Hornby, N. (1995). *High Fidelity.* London: Penguin Books.

Hunt, S. (2005). *The Life Course: A Sociological Introduction.* Basingstoke, UK: Palgrave.

Jefferson, T. (1976). Cultural Responses of the Teds: The Defense of Space. In S. Hall and T. Jefferson (eds.), *Resistance Through Rituals* (pp. 81–86). London: Routledge.

Jenkins, R. (1983). *Lads, Citizens and Ordinary Kids: Working Class Youth Lifestyles in Belfast*. London: Routledge and Kegan Paul.

Jordan, J. (1998). The Art of Necessity: The Subversive Imagination of Anti-Road Protest and Reclaim the Streets. In G. McKay (ed.), *DiY Culture: Party and Protest in Nineties Britain* (pp. 129–251). London: Verso.

Kaplan, E. A. (1987). *Rocking around the Clock: Music Television, Postmodernism and Consumer Culture*. London: Methuen.

Kibby, M. D. (2000). Home on the Page: A Virtual Place of Music Community. *Popular Music*, 19(1): 91–100.

Kompare, D. (2004). Extraordinarily Ordinary: The Osbournes as "An American Family." In S. Murray and L. Ouellette (eds.), *Reality TV: Remaking Television Culture* (pp. 97–118). New York: New York University Press.

Kotarba, J. A. (1994). The Postmodernization of Rock 'n' Roll Music: The Case of Metallica. In J. Epstein (ed.), *Adolescents and Their Music: If It's Too Loud You're Too Old* (pp. 141–163). New York: Garland.

———. (2002). Rock 'n' Roll Music as a Timepiece. *Symbolic Interaction*, 25(3): 397–404.

Laing, D. (1985). *One Chord Wonders: Power and Meaning in Punk Rock*. Milton Keynes, UK: Open University Press.

———. (2004). The Three Woodstocks and the Live Music Scene. In A. Bennett (ed.), *Remembering Woodstock*. Aldershot, UK: Ashgate.

Langlois, T. (1992). Can you feel it? DJs and house music culture in the UK. *Popular Music*, 11(2): 229–238.

Langmead, J. (1994, February 27). Livin' dull. *The Sunday Times—Style and Travel Supplement*, p. 18.

Lee, S. S., and Peterson, R. A. (2004). Internet-Based Virtual Music Scenes: The Case of P2 in Alt.Country Music. In A. Bennett and R. A. Peterson (eds.), *Music Scenes: Local, Translocal, and Virtual*. Nashville, TN: Vanderbilt University Press.

Leech, K. (1973). *Youthquake: The Growth of a Counter-Culture through Two Decades*. London: Sheldon Press.

Lindberg, J. (2007). *Punk Rock Dad: No Rules, Just Real Life*. New York: HarperCollins.

Lipsitz, G. (1994). We Know What Time It Is: Race, Class and Youth Culture in the Nineties. In A. Ross and T. Rose (eds.), *Microphone Fiends: Youth Music and Youth Culture* (pp. 17–28). London: Routledge.

Lull, J. (1992). Popular Music and Communication: An Introduction. In J. Lull (ed.), *Popular Music and Communication* (2nd ed.) (pp. 1–32). London: Sage.

———. (1995). *Media, Communication, Culture: A Global Approach.* Cambridge, UK: Polity Press.

Lurie, A. (1981). *The Language of Clothes.* London: Heinemann.

Macan, E. (1997). *Rocking the Classics: English Progressive Rock and the Counterculture.* Oxford, UK: Oxford University Press.

Macbeth, J. (1992). Ocean cruising: A sailing subculture. *Sociological Review,* 40(2): 319–343.

Maffesoli, M. (1996). *The Time of the Tribes: The Decline of Individualism in Mass Society.* London: Sage.

Malbon, B. (1999). *Clubbing: Dancing, Ecstasy and Vitality.* London: Routledge.

Martin, B. (1998). *Listening to the Future: The Time of Progressive Rock.* Chicago: Open Court.

Martin, Greg (2002). Conceptualizing cultural politics in subcultural and social movement studies. *Social Movement Studies,* 1(1): 73–88.

Martin, G., and Hornsby, J. (1979). *All You Need Is Ears.* London: Macmillan.

Martin, L., and Segrave, K. (1993). *Anti-Rock: The Opposition to Rock 'n' Roll.* New York: Da Capo Press.

Maylon, T. (1998). Tossed in the Fire and They Never Got Burned: The Exodus Collective. In G. McKay (ed.), *DiY Culture: Party and Protest in Nineties Britain* (pp. 187–207). London: Verso.

McDonald-Walker, S. (1998). Fighting the legacy: British bikers in the 1990s. *Sociology,* 32 (2): 379–396.

McGuigan, J. (1992). *Cultural Populism.* London: Routledge.

———. (1999). *Modernity and Postmodern Culture.* Buckingham, UK: Open University Press.

McHugh, K. E. (2003). Three faces of ageism: Society, image and place. *Ageing and Society,* 23(2): 165–185.

McKay, G. (1996). *Senseless Acts of Beauty: Cultures of Resistance since the Sixties.* London: Verso.

———. (ed.). (1998). *DiY Culture: Party and Protest in Nineties Britain.* London: Verso.

———. (2000). *Glastonbury: A Very English Fair.* London: Victor Gollancz.

McRobbie, A. (1990). *Feminism and Youth Culture.* Basingstoke: Macmillan.

———. (ed.) (1994). *Postmodernism and Popular Culture.* London: Routledge.

McRobbie, A., and Garber, J. (1991) Girls and Subcultures. In A. McRobbie (ed.), *Feminism and Youth Culture.* Basingstoke: Macmillan.

Melechi, A. (1993). The Ecstasy of Disappearance. In S. Redhead (ed.), *Rave Off: Politics and Deviance in Contemporary Youth Culture* (pp. 29–40). Aldershot, UK: Avebury.

Melly, G. (1970). *Revolt into Style: The Pop Arts in Britain.* London: Allen Lane.

Michel, S. (2005). M. Crüe catalog. *Spin,* May: 35–36.

Miles, S. (2000). *Youth Lifestyles in a Changing World*. Buckingham, UK: Open University Press.

Mitchell, T. (1996). *Popular Music and Local Identity: Rock, Pop and Rap in Europe and Oceania*. London: Leicester University Press.

Monbiot, G. (1998). Reclaim the Fields and the Country Lanes! The Land Is Ours Campaign. In G. McKay (ed.), *DiY Culture: Party and Protest in Nineties Britain*. London: Verso.

Moore, K., and Haralambous, B. (2007). Barriers to reducing the use of restraints in residential elder care facilities. *Journal of Advanced Nursing*, 58: 532–540.

Mort, F. (1996). *Cultures of Consumption: Masculinities and Social Space in Late Twentieth-Century Britain*. London: Routledge.

Muggleton, D. (2000). *Inside Subculture: The Postmodern Meaning of Style*. Oxford, UK: Berg.

Muggleton, D., and Weinzierl, R. (eds.). (2003). *The Post-Subcultures Reader*. Oxford, UK: Berg.

Negus, K. (1992). *Producing Pop: Culture and Conflict in the Popular Music Industry*. London: Edward Arnold.

O'Connor, A. (2002). Punks and Globalization: Mexico City and Toronto. In P. Kennedy and V. Roudometof (eds.), *Communities across Borders: New Immigrants and Transnational Cultures* (pp. 143–155). London: Routledge.

O'Donnell, H. (2000). Beyond the Modern and the Postmodern: European Soap Operas and Their Adverts. In R. Warner, J. Cannon, and P. Odber (eds.), *Advertising and Identity in Europe: The I of the Beholder* (pp. 121–129). Bristol, UK: Intellect.

Osgerby, B. (2008). Understanding the "Jackpot Market": Media, Marketing and the Rise of the American Teenager. In P. Jamieson and D. Romer (eds.), *The Changing Portrayal of Adolescents in the Media and Why It Matters* (pp. 27–58). New York: Oxford University Press.

Palmer, T. (1976). *All You Need Is Love: The Story of Popular Music*. London: Futura.

Peterson, R. A., and Bennett, A. (2004). Introducing Music Scenes. In A. Bennett, and R. A. Peterson (eds.), *Music Scenes: Local, Translocal, and Virtual* (pp. 1–15). Nashville, TN: Vanderbilt University Press.

Pickering, M. (2001). *Stereotyping: The Politics of Representation*. Basingstoke, UK: Palgrave.

Plasketes, G. M., and Plasketes, J. C. (1987). From Woodstock Nation to Pepsi Generation: Reflections on Rock Culture and the State of Music, 1969–Present. *Popular Music and Society*, 2(2): 25–52.

Polhemus, T. (1997). *Style Surfing: What to Wear in the 3rd Millennium*. New York: Thames and Hudson.

Reading, N., and Appleby, C. (1990). *Are You Experienced? The Inside Story of the Jimi Hendrix Experience*. London: Picador/Pan.

Redhead, S. (1990). *The End-of-the-Century Party: Youth and Pop Towards 2000*. Manchester, UK: Manchester University Press.

———. (1993). The End of the End-of-the-Century Party. In S. Redhead (ed.), *Rave Off: Politics and Deviance in Contemporary Youth Culture* (pp. 1–28). Aldershot, UK: Avebury.

Reich, C. A. (1971). *The Greening of America*. Middlesex, UK: Allen Lane.

Reimer, B. (1995). Youth and Modern Lifestyles. In J. Fornäs and G. Bolin (eds.), *Youth Culture in Late Modernity* (pp. 125–148). London: Sage.

Riesman, D., Glazer, N., and Denny, R. ([1950] 2001). *The Lonely Crowd*. New Haven, CT: Yale University Press.

Rojek, C. (2005). PP2 leisure exchange: Net banditry and the policing of intellectual property. *Leisure Studies*, 24(4): 357–369.

Ross, A. (1994). Introduction. In A. Ross and T. Rose (eds.), *Microphone Fiends: Youth Music and Youth Culture* (pp. 1–13). London: Routledge.

Roszak, T. (1969). *The Making of a Counter Culture: Reflections on the Technocratic Society and Its Youthful Opposition*. London: Faber and Faber.

Rothenbuhler, E. W., and McCourt, T. (1992). Commercial Radio and Popular Music: Processes of Selection and Factors of Influence. In J. Lull (ed.), *Popular Music and Communication* (pp. 78–95). Newbury Park, CA: Sage.

Ryan, J., and Peterson, R. A. (2001). The Guitar as Artifact and Icon: Identity Formation in the Babyboom Generation. In A. Bennett and K. Dawe (eds.), *Guitar Cultures* (pp. 1–14) Oxford, UK: Berg.

Savage, J. (1990). The Enemy Within: Sex, Rock and Identity. In S. Frith (ed.), *Facing the Music: Essays on Pop, Rock and Culture* (2nd ed.) (pp. 131–172). London: Mandarin.

———. (1992). *England's Dreaming: Sex Pistols and Punk Rock*. London: Faber and Faber.

Shank, B. (1994). *Dissonant Identities: The Rock 'n' Roll Scene in Austin, Texas*. London: Wesleyan University Press.

Shields, R. (1991). *Places on the Margin: Alternative Geographies of Modernity*. London: Routledge.

Shuker, R. (2001). *Understanding Popular Music* (2nd ed.). London: Routledge.

Shumway, D. (1992). Rock and Roll as a Cultural Practice. In A. DeCurtis (ed.), *Present Tense: Rock and Roll and Culture*. Durham, NC: Duke University Press.

Smith, J. (2001). Popular Songs and Comic Allusion in Contemporary Cinema. In P. Robertson Wojcik and A. Knight (eds.), *Soundtrack Available: Essays on Film and Popular Music* (pp. 407–430). Durham, NC: Duke University Press.

Smith, N. (2006). Relocating Records, Reconfiguring Age: Adulthood, Identity and the British Northern Soul Scene. Unpublished paper presented at the annual conference of the U.S. branch of the International Association for the Study of Popular Music (IASPM), Middle Tennessee State University, Murfreesboro, TN, February 16–19, 2006.

Smith, P. (2004). *Two of Us: The Story of a Father, a Son and the Beatles*. Boston: Houghon Mifflin Company.

Smith, R. J., and Maughan, T. (1998). Youth culture and the making of the post-Fordist economy: Dance music in contemporary Britain. *Journal of Youth Studies*, 1(2): 211–228.

Spring, K. (2004). Behind the Rave: Structure and Agency in a Rave Scene. In A. Bennett and R. A. Peterson (eds.), *Music Scenes: Local, Translocal, and Virtual* (pp. 48–63). Nashville, TN: University of Vanderbilt Press.

Stahl, G. (2004). "It's Like Canada Reduced": Setting the Scene in Montreal. In A. Bennett and K. Kahn-Harris (eds.), *After Subculture: Critical Studies in Contemporary Youth Culture* (pp. 51–64) London: Palgrave.

Stone, C. J. (1999). *The Last of the Hippies*. London: Faber and Faber.

Stratton, J. (1986). Why doesn't anybody write about glam rock? *The Australian Journal of Cultural Studies*, 4(1): 15–38.

Straw, W. (1991). Systems of articulation, logics of change: Communities and scenes in popular music. *Cultural Studies*, 5(3): 368–388.

———. (1997). Sizing Up Record Collections: Gender and Connoisseurship in Rock Music Culture. In S. Whiteley (ed.), *Sexing the Groove: Popular Music and Gender*. New York: Routledge.

Street, J. (2004). "This Is Your Woodstock": Popular Memories and Political Myths. In A. Bennett (ed.), *Remembering Woodstock*. Aldershot, UK: Ashgate.

Strinati, D. (1995). *An Introduction to Theories of Popular Culture*. London: Routledge.

Stump, P. (1997). *The Music's All That Matters: A History of Progressive Rock*. London: Quartet Books.

Sweeting, A. (1994, October 10). Wall of sound. *The Guardian*, pp. 8–9.

Szemere, A. (1992). The Politics of Marginality: A Rock Musical Subculture in Socialist Hungary in the Early 1980s. In R. Garofalo (ed.), *Rockin' the Boat: Mass Music and Mass Movements*. Boston: South End Press.

Thomas, H. (2003). *The Body, Dance and Cultural Theory*. Basingstoke, UK: Palgrave.

Thompson, H. S. (1993). *Fear and Loathing in Las Vegas*. London: Flamingo.

Thornton, S. (1995). *Club Cultures: Music, Media and Subcultural Capital*. Cambridge, UK: Polity Press.

Timmer, E., Bode, C., and Dittman-Kohl, F. (2003). Expectations of gains in the second half of life: A study of personal conceptions of enrichment in a life-span perspective. *Ageing and Society*, 23(1): 3–24.

Tsitsos, W. (1999). Rules of rebellion: Slamdancing, moshing, and the American alternative scene. *Popular Music*, 18(3): 397–414.

Vroomen, L. (2004). Kate Bush: Teen Pop and Older Female Fans. In A. Bennett and R. A. Peterson (eds.), *Music Scenes: Local, Translocal, and Virtual* (pp. 96–112). Nashville, TN: Vanderbilt University Press.

Walser, R. (1993). *Running with the Devil: Power, Gender and Madness in Heavy Metal Music*. London: Wesleyan University Press.

Waters, C. (1981). Badges of half-formed, inarticulate radicalism: A critique of recent trends in the study of working class youth culture. *International Labor and Working Class History*, 19: 23–37.

Webster, C. (1976). Communes: A Thematic Typology. In S. Hall and T. Jefferson (eds.), *Resistance through Rituals: Youth Subcultures in Post-War Britain* (pp. 127–134). London: Hutchinson.

Weinstein, D. (2000). *Heavy Metal: The Music and Its Culture* (2nd ed.). New York: Da Capo Press.

Willis, P. (1978). *Profane Culture*. London: Routledge and Kegan Paul.

Wise, P. (2006). Australia's Gold Coast: A City Producing Itself. In C. Lindner (ed.), *Urban Space and City Scapes: Perspectives from Modern and Contemporary Culture* (pp. 177–191). London: Routledge.

Wolfe, T. (1968). *The Electric Kool-Aid Acid Test*. New York: Bantam Books.

Wood, R. T. (1999). "Nailed to the X": A lyrical history of the straightedge youth subculture. *Journal of Youth Studies*, 2(2): 133–152.

———. (2003). The straightedge youth sub-culture: Observations on the complexity of sub-cultural identity. *Journal of Youth Studies*, 6(1): 33–52.

Zweig, F. (1961). *The Worker in an Affluent Society: Family Life and Industry*. London: Heinemann.

Index

Andy Bennett is Professor of Cultural Sociology and Director of the Griffith Centre for Cultural Research at Griffith University in Queensland, Australia. He is a Faculty Fellow with the Center for Cultural Sociology at Yale University and author of *Culture and Everyday Life, Cultures of Popular Music,* and *Popular Music and Youth Culture: Music, Identity, and Place.*